Reflections on Speech

A Collection of Essays
by Sam Lessin 2014 – 2019

 The Information

First Edition

Contents

1: Preface

Since I left Facebook in 2014 I have written more columns for The Information about the future of speech then nearly all other topics combined.

The reason is simple. I believe the question of how we engage with and manage the new realities of technological speech is the single most important set of issues we will wrestle with this century, and the issues are both complicated and poorly understood.

The debates around the future of speech and its limits is what we will be remembered for.

That isn't to discredit other major challenges we face, but it is to assert three things that are particularly important about the speech challenges of the day:

The first is that speech if fundamental to not just how we organize our societies, but literally how we conceive of ourselves as people. Speech, memory, and thought are an inseparable bundle that together define us as individuals and how we relate to each other and the rest of the world. When technology impacts speech, it is fundamentally impacting how we think and how we understand our own humanity. Nothing is more fundamental.

The second is that the changes we are experiencing with technological speech are particularly deep and all encompassing. The new super-powers we have with the internet - the ability to instantly and freely speak to and listen to anyone on earth, and remember everything - are a sudden and major break from the historical norm.

Calling the internet an acceleration of the printing press simply does not do it justice.

What we are experiencing is a shift on the level of the invention of speech or perhaps writing, but instead of the change being gradually adopted over millennia – we are experiencing the shift in a single generation.

So, in a sense, of course things have gone crazy.

The third is that when it comes to big technological shifts, the sad reality is that the generation alive during the invention and deployment of the new tools end up being the generation that sets the rules for their use long into the future. Our problematic electrical grid, road infrastructure, and city design are all examples of this challenge.

Future generations consistently get stuck living with the infrastructure choices made by people concurrent with the 'revolution' whether or not those people were actually prepared or informed to make those decisions for the long term. Once rules are set and infrastructure is built, it is nearly impossible to replace.

Given these three points, as I see it, for better and worse our generation is going to be the ones setting the norms and rules which will govern some of the most fundamental human infrastructure imaginable for generations to come.

It is a huge responsibility.

We will almost certainly make big mistakes for which we will be criticized centuries from now; however, we owe it to the world to try to do serious thinking and work with a long-term orientation and not succumb to our immediate fears and interests. As an optimist, I believe that if we take the gravity of what we are doing seriously we can do right by the future.

In a best – if admittedly grandiose – view, maybe we can do as well as the framers of the constitution did in their time of disruption.

What follows in this book is a set of essays which I wrote for The Information over the last several years on the topic of speech. It isn't everything I have written on the topic - and importantly omits the essays I wrote and talks I gave on privacy before joining Facebook in 2010 - but I believe that this set taken together pretty fully represents my views.

I recognize that few people will choose to wade through the full body of work here, so let me orient around three different touch-points for those that are looking to browse.

If you are looking for a reasonably compact and complete snapshot of my view of what has happened with speech on the internet and the path forward, start with 14: How the

<u>Internet Broke and What to Do About It.</u> This single essay was an attempt to wrap up my framework in a single post, so while longer than other essays it is the most complete.

If you are looking for perspectives on the current environment of political speech in the United States generally, and around the upcoming 2020 election in particular, I would suggest starting with <u>4: Free Speech and Democracy in the Age of Micro-Targeting</u>. This 2016 essay anticipated and contextualizes the debate we are having today in 2019 about freedom of speech and advertising for the 2020 election. It also had a major direct impact on some of the changes that Facebook made around political ads disclosure in the last several years.

If you are looking for insight into the next big issue which is currently not in the mainstream press, but I can nearly guarantee will be in the next few years I would start by skimming one of the following: <u>16: A Warning on the Dangers of Ephemeral Messaging</u> , <u>5: The Future of Truth</u> , <u>8: Blockchains and the Right to Be Forgotten</u> , <u>15: How Political Content Fills the Void Left by Micro-Targeting</u>

I hope you enjoy…

— Sam

2: The First Modern Election

November 7, 2016

We just witnessed the first fully modern campaign cycle. If you are versed in science fiction, it played out exactly as predicted. It wasn't pretty.

The public discussion about technology's impact on the election has mostly centered on the direct-to-consumer populism of Donald Trump on social media, but this goes way beyond Twitter and Facebook. The real story is about what it means to operate a democracy in a world of perfect memory and free communication.

THE TAKEAWAY
The advent of recorded history and the rise of free media have reshaped this election and should force us to consider some extreme solutions.

The first reason this cycle has been different is that there is a lot more access to history today than there has been in the past. Henry Kissinger has warned for years about how the transparency of the modern era is destroying diplomacy and the effectiveness of diplomats. This election seems to be proving his point.

Hillary Clinton has been dogged throughout the campaign by email records—those on her private server and those found by WikiLeaks—which didn't exist as a recorded medium even a few decades ago. In a world where business was done face-to-face and through letters, scandals were easily concealed. It's not that there wasn't questionable behavior before. There was just no accessible record of it.

Trump's campaign has been similarly forced to deal with new forms of recorded history. Setting aside tax records, there was the infamous Access Hollywood tape and remarks to Howard Stern. In an earlier era, most of his historical transgressions would have been debatable hearsay of partial recollections. Today they are recorded irrefutable fact.

And I suspect the campaigns have probably capitalized on this, pacing their release of recorded "history" for maximal impact. This changes the strategy of campaigning to focus more on the past than the future.

Of course, this isn't just about the internet and computers. Xerox, which turned the copying of records into a cultural norm, has only been around since the 1960s. Personal history just isn't that old. Candidates up until very recently have had at most a small percentage of their lives recorded.

Forgetting the Future

How are we going to deal with a world where the only candidates without recorded foibles are the ones with no history at all?

For a long time there has been a question of whether a world in which everything is transparent will make us more open or turn us into repressed automatons.

I would argue that most signs point toward transparency making us as people more open, honest and forgiving. Even at the presidential level we went, in one generation, from "I did not inhale" to it being perfectly acceptable that Obama experimented with cocaine.

But, when it comes to a split nation and derisive politics, perfect memory is either going to outright disqualify most candidates for high office, or make it so unappealing to run that no one talented and sane is going to bother.

We have to come to terms with the fact that if everything is remembered, there will be tons of unflattering stuff available on everyone. Of course, not all embarrassing stuff is equal, and we have to learn to forgive some things without excusing the unforgivable.

We also have to learn how to have a conversation about the future when the past is both so mesmerizing and easily at hand.

Instant Free Communication

The second factor that makes this election cycle truly modern is the media the candidates have received at zero incremental cost.

Facebook and Twitter are part of the story—but only a small part. After all, while we have been inundated with Trump, he only has 12.9 million Twitter followers and 11 million Facebook likes—and let's be honest about the percentage of those that are likely bots. Jessica made a good point about the impact of something as basic as email in her post on Friday.

As the candidates have gained access to unmediated direct forms of communication through social, email and video, they have brought the bulk of the rest of the media, and the discussion, along with them at zero incremental cost.

Hillary Clinton has been dogged throughout the campaign by email records—those on her private server and those found by WikiLeaks—which didn't exist as a recorded medium even a few decades ago.

One way to think about this is to recognize just how little each candidate actually spent this cycle to get their message out to the whole country. According to the Washington Post, Hillary has raised $1.3 billion

($556 million directly to the campaign). Trump has raised $795 million ($248 million directly to the campaign).

While those numbers might seem large, remember that the most generous view of the Democrats' spending on the campaign is basically $4.30 per American, or less than 30 minutes of work at the California state minimum wage.

Or, if you want to compare the numbers to private tech company fundraising, the Hillary campaign has raised half of what Snapchat has raised to date and just about a third of what Uber has raised last summer alone. That is a pittance for control of an $18 trillion economy.

The reason that the numbers are so low relative to the impact is that the bulk of the actual "financing" for both campaigns has come through readily accessible free media, where the currency that sells is extremism, not reason or honest debate. It is the echo chamber of Fox and CNN that is permanently "breaking news," along with the newspapers and the radio stations scraping for pennies as their business models crumble, that are providing all the real financing for the campaigns.

So, campaigns are cheaper to run than ever, and the media, without any meaningful remaining control over distribution, is forced to kowtow to extremism. Facebook and Twitter might represent the spearhead that is morphing the rest of the public discourse in their wake, but they are just the tip of the spear, not the whole story.

The Transition Isn't Over

What are we to do about it all? Here are two scary ideas.

To deal with the race to the bottom of instant free communication, we might have to start making it unprofitable for attention-driven, advertising-supported platforms to cover politics. One idea would be to force news platforms to give back to the government a percentage of their revenue in proportion to the amount of time they spend covering candidates—a coverage tax. It wouldn't be insane for CNN to give 50% of its revenue to the government because 50% of their content is election coverage.

That would basically say that you can't profit off the public discourse at all. We the people own it. (Covering private industry is another matter.)

If that isn't sufficiently strange to consider, let's talk about how to destroy history to save the republic.

It is already possible to manipulate video and audio so that people will be able to credibly forge visual and audio history of events that never happened.

A world where anyone can create a fake video of anyone else saying almost anything is almost too cataclysmic to our way of interacting to contemplate.

But it would take care of the issue of us being overly fixated on history; it would be impossible to trust most of what you see and hear as truth. People would rapidly get bored of talking about it and focus instead on coming up with sound plans for the future.

This is obviously crazy, and not a world I necessarily want to see myself. But, the reality is that the ultimate solution to privacy is almost certainly robust misinformation, not trying to hide information anymore. The modern way to destroy information is by hiding it in even more information.

That's a scenario Kissinger probably never contemplated but that could prove his words even more true.

3: The Rise of Information Imperialism

November 21, 2016

It recently dawned on me that we are in an age of information imperialism. Small communities of people used to have their own private stores of knowledge that were distinct to their local communities. That local knowledge defined and bonded them.

The internet broadly has opened all of those local pockets and connected everyone and their knowledge to a powerful global infrastructure, not unlike how the railroad and steamships of the 19th century connected the globe. And, in so doing, it has destroyed a lot of these local communities.

THE TAKEAWAY
The internet is turning out to be a disaster for information diversity, contrary to widespread opinion among the technorati. The more seductive ideas crowd out niche opinions. The danger is that it's now possible for the government to regulate actual speech.

With the election of Trump and a wave of anti-globalization, we now have to have a serious conversation in practical terms about the ills that come with a world of open and free communication.

Destruction of Local Knowledge

I was thinking about these issues the other day while biking through San Francisco and up around Marin. If you unwound the clock even 20 years, and took away Google Maps, it would be difficult for me—as a casual biker—to figure my way out around some of the winding best bike routes in the region. Only people in the biking community in the area would know their way around. Now, with technology, it is easy—and that means the best bike routes are far more popular and crowded.

Broader access to knowledge of a place, person, thing or topic changes the thing itself. Just like in quantum physics, our new tools that allow us to observe the information, in many instances destroys it—or at least its value.

What is destroyed when a local community's special information is shared?

First, without knowledge as a barrier to access, what is generally left is just money, and that creates social stress.

The events business is an interesting example here. It used to be that even if you wanted to buy courtside seats to a great game, being deep enough in the community to know how to buy those tickets was hard. You couldn't just buy your way into whatever you wanted—you also needed knowledge and information about the community of the team. Now, of course, access to the best tickets at any sporting event or concert is just a matter of money in a liquid market. In some ways, erasing information as a barrier is a very good thing for the world. There is an argument that it is more fair and open that way, but there is something lost from the community when the only currency is money. And, I would argue, it also creates more anxiety about money itself.

Second, information imperialism—defined as the opening up of the world's knowledge—is a knowledge-diversity disaster. If all ideas compete for attention and engagement in an open marketplace, the most seductive ideas are more powerful. That means it is less possible for niche ideas to stand their ground with locally relevant audiences. This suggests that as the internet opens up all knowledge and speech, we actually end up with less diversity of ideas and opinions. We bias more toward monocultures versus polycultures, and toward a more fragile information ecology.

Suggesting that the internet squashes rather than promotes diversity is heresy among the technorati. The narrative is supposed to be that the internet gives everyone a voice, and lets each voice find its audience. Do we see that happening? What I see is that certain voices, a Trump or a Kanye West or a

Kim Kardashian, get far, far more attention than they did in the past, crowding out other views and speech.

Broader access to knowledge of a place, person, thing or topic changes the thing itself.

Sure, there are more TV shows and more selfies of different people. But from a macro sense, are we seeing growth in diversity of ideas or consolidation? It might be that our ability to more seamlessly spread ideas and memes is actually collapsing our global diversity of ideas, not expanding it.

Third, our global network opens up, for the first time in human history, the real possibility that freedom of knowledge and speech will be removed. Historically, while different societies have had different opinions around the protection of freedom of speech, there was a practical limit on enforcement. A government or organization might prevent the mass distribution of an idea, but it was functionally impossible to regulate the actual local speech and knowledge of a community. You simply couldn't monitor speech at the local level. It was impossible.

Our global network has changed this. I am not an alarmist: I trust our government and the organizations that oversee the internet. However, it is now possible for the government, or another organization, to regulate what we can and can't say. This is why the suggestion of things like Facebook "editorializing" News Feed, hiring human journalists and behaving like a media organization is so fundamentally flawed and scary. Those asking for it, mostly very shortsighted "liberals," are heading toward a slippery slope that leads to the demise of possibly our most important freedom.

Where Do We Go From Here?

Globalization in the 19th century was both terribly destructive and very good. For all the pain, suffering and destruction it caused, no one in their right mind would want to unwind the clock for humanity overall.

The same I believe is true for the globalization of information, and our current period of information imperialism. It has terrible effects, but it is also a net good. We can't turn back time, but even if we could, we absolutely shouldn't want to.

That said, I think it is very much worth understanding and acknowledging what we are doing, and that the internet is not all good. It comes with costs. Only when you confront the ways in which it has distorted local communities, destroyed diversity and posed new risks to free speech can we move forward with our eyes wide open into the future.

The internet is good, but it isn't all good.

4: Free Speech and Democracy in the Age of Micro-Targeting

December 5, 2016

or many centuries philosophers, political scientists and lawyers have taken for granted that there is a reasonably clear distinction between the public and private spheres and the nature of "speech" in each space.

The private sphere—i.e., speaking with friends in your home—was a sphere of very limited audience and unlimited speech. You were free to say on- or off-the-record almost anything you wanted, but your audience was limited to the people you could pack in your living room.

THE TAKEAWAY
The growth of micro-targeting and disappearing messaging on the internet means that politicians can say different things to large numbers of people individually, in a way that can't be monitored. Requirements to put this discourse on the public record are required to maintain democracy.

This stood in stark contrast to the public sphere—speaking on a stage or to a mass audience through a broadcast—where your audience could be of almost unlimited size. But your speech was limited to the messages which would appeal to a diversity of people and you had to be OK with everyone knowing what you said.

In its first iteration, the largely anonymous internet of webpages looked like a simple, if powerful, extension of the public sphere. It allowed individuals to speak to more people than previous mediums did, on a far wider diversity of topics.

But, as the internet has become ever more personalized, it increasingly represents a strange hybrid of the public and private spheres. Through micro-targeting and customization, the internet now provides the opportunity for people to reach an unlimited audience with unlimited speech.

If there is, therefore, a conversation to be had about the impact of the internet on the election, it shouldn't be about fake news and feed ranking (which I believe are red herrings). It should be about what it means that a public candidate can for the first time effectively talk to each individual voter privately in their own home and tell them exactly what they want to hear.

Clearly, this merging of the public and private spheres represents a new space for speech which is powerful, personalized and un-audited. We clearly don't yet have good frameworks for managing this space. And, frankly, we need as a society to get a grip on managing it if we want democracy to thrive going forward.

The Technology Tools of Mass Private Speech

Mass private speech isn't entirely new. Phone banking, where people dial a pre-determined list on a candidate's behalf, is a crude, low-data form of a candidate talking privately with a string of individuals through a surrogate. Phone banking is expensive to run, though. And because intermediate people make phone calls on your behalf, the customization of your message can't be very personalized.

Good old-fashioned mail and email have also been micro-targeting tools for a long time. The companies and movements that have the best data and are best at targeting can present themselves in massively different ways to different people.

Recently, there has been some attention paid to Facebook page posts, both free and sponsored, which can be limited with audience restrictions to only show specific messages to specific people. This is a powerful evolution from prior tools and there are good reasons for the product to exist. If you are a brand like Nike with a global voice you obviously want to be able to deliver different messages to people in the U.S. versus the U.K. And you want to deliver messages in French to people in France and in German to people in Germany. You also likely want to be able to target messages differently for men and women, and based on interests in different sports. This is how brands work when they buy ads in different cities or against different TV shows—it's just far more effective with Facebook's data.

Of course, once you open up the ability to customize whom you are speaking to, it is easy to go further with micro-targeting. Brands want a way of—and get a lot of value from—marrying data with purchase histories, web traffic, email directories, ad nauseum, etc. Of course, so do sophisticated politicians who know how to use the tools.

Customized Facebook ads and page posts might be easy to see as technology of mass private speech, but they are hardly the only tools at play. Most websites, which once showed more or less the same content to everyone, are now hyper-personalized based on your interaction history, interests and the tracking pixels all over the web. With rare exceptions like Wikipedia, what you see and what I see when I visit webpages is massively different—whether we are on SoundCloud or BuzzFeed.

Disappearing messages on Snapchat and Instagram only further exacerbate this trend. They allow messages to not only be targeted to specific people, but give the speaker the ability to make it difficult for the recipient to screenshot or share the message they are presenting. The privacy-oriented features that might have been originally intended to give teens the feeling of safety to speak more freely to their friends also have major payoffs to public figures who want more freedom in the extreme messages they are dispatching to individuals. These features allow speech to not only be personalized, but make it almost impossible for the speech to be audited by outsiders.

Next up likely will at some point be experiences with conversation agents and perhaps in things like VR. Your virtual reality experience, powered by intimate knowledge of who you are, will be very different from mine. When I talk to a chatbot, the suggestions it will make to me will increasingly diverge from what it says when you talk to the same chatbot.

The upshot is simple. Lots of data, and systems which can react properly to the interests, beliefs, and feelings of different people lead to a world where technology and brands tell us exactly what we want to hear in a way that can't be tracked or audited. Tools intended originally to give individuals a more private space to share with friends are easily co-opted by public figures looking to speak in more extremes. And just as critically, we have absolutely no idea what the same voices are saying to everyone else.

Where Has the Public Sphere Gone?

It is always interesting when a candidate's private speech to a small group of donors leaks to the public. It is a rare glimpse of the targeted message that candidates deliver to a hyper-targeted audience. I have been to events like this, and while I have never heard a "basket of deplorables" line from a candidate in private, I can tell you that they say different things in smaller groups (and are usually way more compelling to their targeted audience).

Through micro-targeting and customization, the internet now provides the opportunity for people to reach an unlimited audience with unlimited speech.

Take that concept, and now imagine that the candidate (or brand)—with good technology and data—can speak to each person individually in their home. They can say whatever they want with reasonable confidence that their words will not leave the room. In a world like this, why would they ever give public speeches or start a public discourse? It would be far better to have a customized and personal message for each person and then say nothing publicly.

I believe, at least in part, that is what we saw in this last election cycle. At a public level, in big speeches broadcast to everyone, neither candidate really said all that much. The debates were shocking mostly due to the fact that there were almost no really deep discussions of policy or viewpoints.

There are rumors that candidates were making bold and aggressive claims to small targeted populations away from the eye of the broad-based public via private, small groups, and one-on-ones, as facilitated by the internet. The challenge is, of course, that because of the nature of the speech it is hard to really know.

That said, it did feel like the goal of the public discussion became to say as little as possible to allow the candidates full breathing room to say in private exactly what they wanted.

The technorati, along with lots of media pundits, have been bemoaning the idea that we now live in "feed bubbles" and "echo chambers" where we only see the viewpoints of like-minded people and miss the broader narrative. To me, feed bubbles was the discussion to have five years ago. The far more complicated and insidious problem of today is personal, private and disappearing messaging that can be powerful but can't be broadly traced or audited.

What to Do

Democracy, so the theory goes, only works with a vibrant public discourse. It requires multiple candidates putting forth to an electorate ideas and positions and competing for votes against one another in public.

If we are entering a world where elections are done via deeply informed, mass one-on-one conversations versus public sphere speeches, what can we do to preserve the discourse?

It would be both silly, and likely impossible, to somehow regulate the use of private speech or micro-targeting in elections. But what we could do is require that all the data and communication from all campaigns must be public record.

If all the data that campaigns use to craft messages for individuals, as well as all the things that candidates say to individuals, were forced to be public record, then at least watchdogs could figure out which people were being fed lies.

This will cause upheaval. It will mean that, at least for political candidates, there can no longer be such a thing as a private fundraiser dinner. It will also mean that anything they say to any individual citizen in private, and the data they collect on individuals, will have to be available to be shared with everyone.

That is a pretty big change from the way the world has worked to date. It basically would mean that candidates need to sacrifice any access to the private sphere they once had.

But, to me, this seems not only feasible but necessary. We cannot allow campaigns to be waged in private.

I believe that we will look back at this period and laugh about our distraction with sideshows like "fake news" and "feed bubbles." The real story of this period is how the internet, and the world, is moving away from feeds and toward private messaging, groups, disappearing messages and closed spaces, and how successful brands (and candidates) are customizing their messages in an un-audited space specifically for those groups—not for re-shares in more public spaces.

5: The Future of Truth

July 31, 2017

For the last century we have had the luxury of being able to rely on photos, video and audio for a recorded understanding of truth. But for most of human history, trust and truth were far more complicated. World events couldn't be directly observed.

Surprisingly, after just a brief period of being able to trust recordings we find ourselves on a clear path back in time. Technology, particularly artificial intelligence, is taking away our ability to directly observe truth. It is becoming as easy to create fake but believable images, video, and even audio as it is to create text with false claims today.

THE TAKEAWAY
AI technologies are making it much easier for people to manipulate video and audio to turn the fake into believable images. To figure out what is true in future, people are going to have to pay more and rely on social networks. Blockchain technologies could help make systems more trustworthy.

In this respect, I oddly agree with Elon Musk. I don't buy his grandstanding about how AI poses a mortal threat to humanity as a sentient or more powerful intelligence. I do believe, however, that AI is increasingly effective at generating highly believable lies. The ease and effectiveness with which we will be able to lie to each other is going to tear at the fabric of our global society in deeply disruptive ways.

The Not Too Distant Future: A World Awash of Fake Video, Audio and Photos

In the last several months videos have been floating around the web showing how video and audio can be easily manipulated to make it appear that almost anyone is saying almost anything. A good recent example, from University of Washington professors, uses former President Barack Obama's speech patterns to demonstrate one form of the technology. Another good demonstration, from Stanford last year, shows face expression-matching research.

In a sense, this isn't new. For a long time, Hollywood studios have been creating believable fakes, bringing back deceased actors or grafting live actors onto increasingly expressive cartoon scaffoldings.

Much like weapons proliferation, however, the ability to create believable fakes isn't too scary when it is extremely time consuming and expensive to access. It is far more dangerous, however, when the technology gets good enough that almost anyone can generate believable fake media with access to the internet, hundreds of dollars of equipment, and a few hours. That's the direction in which we are marching.

We already have some good indications of what this is going to feel like as a consumer. For many years, fake text has been easy to generate and distribute on the internet, with humans writing some content, and bots writing other content. The result is that the open web is largely discredited and un-usable at this point. It is impossible to know what is true or not, which explains at least partially the dramatic fall of the open web and rise of walled gardens.

Perfect Lies and Discredited Reality

It would be one thing if the world evolved in a direction where there were massive amounts of fake but highly believable content, but it was still easy to tell what was truly true. Then this would just be a spam problem. But sadly, one of the things that modern AI techniques is best at is using massive amounts of context to make unreality fully believable.

If you want to viscerally understand this, watch this video demonstrating neural network based photo editing.

Rather than traditional pixel-by-pixel image adjustments, the video demonstrates how using a generative adversarial network-based approach you can make a photo editing system that takes a small amount of input on how you want to manipulate an image, and the system can fill in the rest to make a whole image believable. Rather than needing to perfectly create a fake beard or a different hairstyle, all you need to do is suggest a few pixels of what you want. The system can use knowledge of a large set of real images to back-solve for believability.

In the not-too-distant future, using a data set of real faces (or real video, real audio and speech patterns) you will be able to choose the edit you want to make to a piece of media. Machines will fill in everything you would need to make your content believable.

Fake images aren't new. In the fashion industry today no one trusts the reality of imagery anymore. Even on a consumer level, photo filters and simple retouch tools have made images more about emotion and expression than reality.

But we are rapidly approaching a world where no images can be believed in and of themselves, and the edits people make aren't simply fashion touchups.

Tools for The Future of Truth

There are effectively three problems that we need to solve. The first is identifying what primary sources to trust. The second is extending those networks of trust beyond people and sources we immediately know. The third is how to trust the messaging infrastructure to not corrupt or alter the information we share.

Identifying primary sources to trust is in some ways the easiest problem to solve.

Capitalism is—at its best—a technology of truth. For centuries powerful families and royalty have paid agents all over the globe for accurate information. If you wanted an accurate view of reality, you cultivated and paid a set of people to verify the truth to the best of their abilities. Even if you weren't a Rothchild with your own private sources, there were more accessible journals and newsletters you could buy, and trust were aligned with reality because their value depended on it. It is simple and it works.

In the last 100 years, we frankly have become lazy about this. A world of recorded media —which temporarily made truth easier to understand—has depressed our willingness to pay for trustable information. The emergence of modern advertising created an alternate and seductive framework for paying for information, at least in the short term.

But as the world realigns and truth becomes harder to discern, the simple but pure idea of paying agents for an understanding of truth once again becomes important. You will get what you pay for.

As the world realigns and truth becomes harder to discern, the simple but pure idea of paying agents for an understanding of truth once again becomes important. You will get what you pay for.

Extending Trust Through Social Networks

People love to complain about the spam, scams and lies on things like Facebook. But the reality is that for most people, Facebook provides a far more trustable source of reality than the open web. Using people you trust as the ultimate input to screen for reality is the way trust has worked historically, and digital tools that work along those same lines are critical. If the network of people you listen to is good, your information is good.

Of course, the experience is only as good as the people and things you connect to. Social networking in the digital world, just as it is in the physical world, is a double-edge sword. It is just social infrastructure, so if you are connected to people who aren't trustworthy or want to use the tool in manipulative ways, it will damage your view of reality. And we are still figuring out how to know whom to trust online (particularly if you are connecting to people you don't know in the real world).

Modern social networks also are no longer just the network itself. They have an incentive to want people to share more, and for what gets shared to be more engaging. So there is enormous pressure on the networks to make product design decisions that implicitly or explicitly shape opinions and affects the messages people want to share. This makes them a party to the information, not just the trust relationships, which is a very tenuous relationship at best.

Trusting the Messengers

Even if you have faith in a primary set of sources, and the sanctity of a social network of trust, you have to trust the technical systems in the middle that are delivering your messages. This is where debates over encryption, VPNs, blockchains and maybe someday quantum communication come in.

There was a brief period in time where it felt like— at least in the West—people trusted the sanctity of our messaging infrastructure. For instance, for generations the American people trusted that the mail system was private and secure, with steep legal penalties for opening mail not intended for them.

This is all, sadly, again coming to a head. More players are achieving the technical sophistication to snoop and modify messages passing over the internet, evidenced by things like the fact that China is now able to block images based on content within messenger applications.

There is some good news in things like the rise of blockchains. While the current application of blockchains might be simple registers of accounts and values, the idea of highly distributed databases is going to be important for the future of truth. They allow for a sense of consensus truth where, in theory, no single actor can manipulate or change the group's sense of reality.

The bad news about blockchains is that, just like democracy, truth becomes what the majority of actors in the system believe to be true—not actual reality. The other bad news about blockchains, in their current form, is that while in theory they should be platforms for distributed truth, in practice there is a large incentive for the consolidation of power into a small number of hands who aggregate a lot of the compute power that makes them secure. Just like social networking, there is a tendency toward consolidation.

In the end, the future of trusting messengers in the middle of communications flows is going to have to be, first, "wires" secured with encryption—and maybe even someday quantum technology (though that will be both extremely difficult and highly controlled by governments). And second, tamper-proof databases, which probably resemble highly distributed databases spread out using blockchains.

The Tower of Babel

Personally I am very disquieted about my inability to know whom to trust these days. There are extremely important issues like global warming where polarized news sources with conflicted agendas make it hard to know whether we are facing issues on a 20- or 200-year basis. As an American, I still mostly trust the formal layers of communication I use. But if I lived in many countries on Earth I would no longer trust the network itself.

It is hard not to think of the story of the Tower of Babel when evaluating the current situation. For a while, the internet looked like a grand project bringing the world together and allowing us all to coordinate on important human-scale projects, like combatting global warming.

Just like in the story of the Tower of Babel, however, just as we started using a common language, something came along and scattered the languages and trust. The internet regionalized and centralized, people lost a sense of whom to trust, and in so doing a lot of the coordination power we once had.

I am still an optimist. With the right incentives for primary sources, strong social networking technology, and good encryption and distribution, I think the internet can still be a major leap forward for a global understanding of truth, trust and our ability to work together.

But it isn't going to be easy. After a honeymoon century where we could trust primary images, video, and audio—and the sanctity of the internet—we are going to have to start working harder for the truth. Technology gives, and technology takes away.

6: The Future of Free Speech

Sept 11, 2017

In the past several years technology has made speech dramatically more powerful and free than was conceivable in the past. In 2017, with a highly charged atmosphere locally and globally, the question of how the concept of freedom of speech is going to modernize is coming to the fore. A key issue is how far big internet platforms like Facebook and YouTube will go to clamp down on extremist speech.

This conversation has flared up in the context of a wave of broadly publicized and deeply polarizing events, running the gamut from Google's dismissal of James Damore to CloudFlare and others dropping Daily Stormer in the wake of Charlottesville to strong language and politics around demonstrations throughout the country.

THE TAKEAWAY
Technology has fundamentally changed the properties of speech in terms of reach and precision, and might require us as a society to re-examine how we approach freedom of speech.

More generally, this conversation is happening amid simmering concerns around the role of social networking and fake news connected to the election in November, flare-ups on many college campuses, questions around the role of money in politics, calls to lock up members of the media, and degraded trust in many governmental, academic and news institutions.

In short, we are sitting on a speech powder keg. It isn't inconceivable that someone will try to change the First Amendment in coming years through a constitutional amendment. Free speech rights also might be challenged by internet service providers or consumer internet firms taking action to block speech some consider offensive.

As this extremely important debate unfolds in the next few years there are several principles that are critical to keep in mind.

Speech is irreversibly super-empowered by technology via both reach and precision

When people talk about the implications of the internet on free speech they usually discuss the enormous unfettered reach that the internet and social media has given individuals. In 1791 when the First Amendment was passed, free speech was understood in terms of people's ability to speak to dozens or hundreds in churches, town halls and bars. It also meant the ability to deliver short pamphlets to thousands if you had the resources and time.

It would be inconceivable to that generation that thousands of people now can—in mere seconds and acting alone—reach out and talk to millions. No prince or king had that ability a few hundred years ago, let alone an ordinary citizen. In this way the reach of the internet is indeed game-changing for the nature of speech. The real-world friction that existed as a counterweight to freedom to speak in the 18th century is gone.

That said, while the scale is new, the reach of individual voices has been growing for a long time, through emergence of radio, film and television. The bigger departure from history caused by the internet is the ability to explicitly include or exclude people from a given discussion. It cannot be understated how big a deal this is, and it goes far beyond questions of newsfeed bias and ad targeting.

In the days before the internet, the expectation was that you could say extreme things and hold extreme views, but that it was very difficult to find a like-minded audience of extremists without simultaneously bringing everyone else into the conversation. You couldn't find the needles in the haystack that agreed with you and wanted to work with you without everyone else knowing what you were saying and doing.

The internet has brought the ability to find dozens of people to agree with or support you out of a pool of millions in private. This is the more disruptive part of our new technology because it can deeply empower extremists without being visible or understood by the broader public.

Of course, it is a double-edge sword. In the best light, the ability to have a private conversation with micro-communities of similarly interested people is what has allowed geek culture to flourish under what was a sea of mass culture. It is what helps people looking for support with rare diseases find each other. It helps create safe spaces for people to organize for change in healthy ways.

But when you wonder how extremist groups are able to find each other and organize protests and counter-protests, recognize that those people had a far harder time finding each other in the sea of moderates in a pre-internet time. While there are a handful of exceptions, in general most could never mass support in any numbers in an era before cheap air travel.

This is the scary legacy of our new communication technology. If speech was originally granted the status of being a "right" in an attempt to prevent the many from oppressing the few, with new technology there is at least an argument that now dozens—with far greater distribution and private organizing power than ever before—can oppress millions.

Consolidated private platforms are challenged with questions of intervention

The second interesting part about our modern landscape is that where once control over speech was distributed among millions of speakers, and hundreds of small publications, it is unquestionable that power over "speech" is now largely consolidated among a few largely unregulated private platforms.

There is a fierce debate over whether this is a good or bad thing. Regardless, what is clear is that large internet companies are now actively engaged in the question of what types of speech they are willing to distribute broadly. YouTube, Facebook and the like have all taken clear stances that certain types of speech are banned from distribution on their platforms, and are using technology to monitor their enormous communities. While they might not be formally regulated, they certainly are weighing the interests of regulators in the context of their actions. We as a society, as proxied by the decisions of large internet companies, are willing to manage the distribution power of the internet.

All that said, the question I really worry about is what are we willing or not willing to do about the precision power of the internet? On that point, we are in uncharted waters.

If you agree that the ability to find and cultivate like-minded micro-minorities is the most powerful and scariest part of speech on the modern internet, at some point we are going to run directly up against the question of what conversations are allowed in private messaging conversations and groups.

This debate is already under way, encoded in the language of "encryption" debates. Apple, WhatsApp and many others have a long history of talking about the sanctity of encryption. For all of human history, regardless of whatever speech laws were on the books, people have had the key freedom to speak privately to each other in families and trusted communities with minimal fear of reprisals. Only the most aggressive regimes have looked to undermine the trust in truly private speech.

The internet challenges that because without encryption, in theory all communication can be monitored—not just public speech.

The question, then, is whether the big platforms in the U.S. will be pressured to clamp down on private speech on services like WhatsApp.

Limits likely won't stop speech but will send it further underground

Let's pretend that we did end up in a world where the big speech-platforms decided to not only limit public broadcast but also private speech. What then?

You won't stop extreme speech or what flows from it. You will simply force it underground and into forms that are basically unstoppable. It's already the case that most of the truly extreme speech occurs not on mainstream platforms but on corners of the internet, and on the dark web. Things like Silk Road or now AlphaBay have existed for a long time and will always exist.

As technology improves this extreme speech will only become harder to disrupt. Even if a lot of the chatter on something like Silk Road was through encryption, it has been possible to "shut it off" technologically. Technologies like blockchains—which allow not just communication but also storage to be more easily distributed—are going to make it basically impossible to limit speech on the internet.

So the question becomes, would you rather have people saying terrible things in private on mainstream platforms, or force more development and more discovery of far darker parts of the internet as people promote and look for alternatives?

Making extreme speech harder to access will prevent some people who might otherwise engage from engaging. But the more that people feel limited the more you might send them off to darker corners of the internet.

Speech is even more charged in a world of digital identity

The implications of this speech debate go far beyond simple questions of communication in a world of deep digital identity.

In the last several months Airbnb and Uber have made it clear that certain types of people, or members of certain groups, will be blocked from using their services. Many people in the mainstream applaud this. As private platforms, the argument is, they have the right to make this decision. It is good PR. And for this is a straightforward way for platforms not oriented around speech to take a stance on a hotly debated social problem of the day.

It is, however, deeply unsettling that these companies even have the ability to block certain types of users, let alone are using it to exclude people from service—and it puts even a higher premium on the issue of speech.

Technology, identity, and power have been deeply associated for a very long time. In the days of Bismarck, new systems and forms of record-keeping allowed for the first time identity-based social services and a powerful war machine. Obviously the Nazi regime's ability to keep records was a key ingredient in their committing crimes against humanity.

The fact that now, non-governmental organizations of massive scale have the information-power to take action against people based on speech obviously raises the stakes. As a society, we need to be in conversation with these organizations. And in a fully connected and largely consolidated world the decisions we make on speech have implications far beyond what they once did.

The Chinese have some form of an answer—with new VPN restrictions and deep learning to peer inside private messaging apps. It is an unappealing answer to those that worry about the tyranny of the majority, but a valid one nonetheless. What new standards will we pick and as a civilization, either recommitting ourselves to free speech with all the terrible rhetoric and conflict that comes from it, or picking some other alternative?

Free speech ultimately is the privilege of a healthy society

My personal perspective is that we have to start recognizing guarantees of free speech as the privilege of a strong and stable society. As the nursery rhyme goes, "stick and stones will break my bones but words will never hurt me."

In the future we aren't going to be able to prevent either consolidation of the conversation or keep people from splintering off and having fringe conversations. Unless we want to outright ban certain types of conversation, which seems like the scariest possible outcome for our way of life, we are going to have to tolerate a communication landscape littered with hateful words from the fringes of society, words which are wrong, poorly expressed and downright scary. That is the part of the bargain we have with freedom today and in the future.

This is the broader challenge of technology. It rearranges all of the barriers of the physical world and challenges the values we have established as rights.

There are specific things we should modify in terms of how we deal with certain types of speech. For example, I strongly believe, as I have written before, that specifically for paid political speech it is imperative that the specific copy and targeting clusters used by campaigns should be part of the public record. I think this is the type of limited and valuable rule we should consider.

But broadly, I hope that as we grow as a society into this new age we move away from shutting off voices from college campuses to protests, and focus on limiting violence— especially intentionally provoked violence.

It would be an enormous triumph for the U.S. to feel secure enough in its identity to be able to tolerate free speech even as the internet accelerates the sometimes terrible reality of what that entails. It would also be the ultimate sign of our health as a civilization.

7: The Tower of Babel: Five Challenges of the Modern Internet

November 6, 2017

Late last year, I wrote a <u>column about free speech</u> and democracy in the age of micro-targeting. In it I observed that in order to preserve an open democratic discourse, it was critical to require that all micro-targeted political ads and their targeting information be public record, so that advocates and watchdog organizations could keep track of what candidates and their supporters were claiming in private at scale to different constituents.

It was heartening to see that almost exactly a year later Facebook has very strongly committed to move to do exactly that, making all ads and most targeting information publicly available for review on pages.

THE TAKEAWAY
- Consolidation of speech platforms poses risks
- Current internet is biased toward extreme speech
- Choices loom about prioritizing freedom vs. security

This was a necessary step, but a year into intense controversy and debate—and on the heels of congressional hearings—it is clear that transparency around paid speech isn't going to be enough. Unfortunately for everyone, the debates around how the internet should and will evolve only get more controversial, pitting core assumptions of our civilization against one another.

By removing the natural friction of communication in the physical world, and allowing mass targeted speech by people (and machines), technology is forcing us to grapple with beliefs that have always sat in balance with one another. Years ago, it was possible to simultaneously value openness and freedom, equality and fairness, and security and stability. The days where the physical friction of reality allowed these ideas to peacefully co-exist are coming to a close, and the internet is forcing us to reconcile their fundamental inconsistency. In a modern, frictionless world, you can't have an open and free world that also is equal as well as secure and stable. Something has to give.

We are going to need to make some very tough decisions in the coming years and prioritize our values in new ways.

Towers to the Heavens

When thinking about the problems we now face as a civilization, I am vividly reminded of the story of the Tower of Babel.

The story, which is mirrored in many different cultures, is that in an earlier time humanity was unified and spoke a common language. As a single force people were able to do great things at scale, and they decided to begin building a tower to the heavens together.

The hubris of trying to build a tower to the heavens threatened God, who, as punishment fractured the language of men and made it impossible for people to understand one another.

It has been a foregone conclusion for a long time in many circles that the internet has been a vehicle for moving us toward speaking one common language and being able to work together to solve the great problems of our era, ranging from global warming, poverty and disease, to ideally aspirational missions like interstellar travel.

As I have discussed before, it also is clear that just as in the story of Babel there is pressure built into the internet's DNA, accelerated by things like artificial intelligence, that threatens to undermine our ability to understand one another, see reality the same way and function on big projects as a unified force.

The sad reality is that the most exciting attempt to bring our world together is putting us at risk of not being able to trust what we see or hear.

What Hard Choices Are We Willing to Make?

As I see it, there are a series of questions that we are going to have to tackle in order to preserve the internet as a functional communications platform, and they are going to require some very deep tradeoffs. We aren't going to get everything we want. But we are going to have to actually make, rather than just intellectually debate, the following decisions:

1. Is Anonymity a Feature to Be Protected, or a Bug to Be Quashed?

The internet started out as a place where you could be someone other than yourself. The ability to be anonymous has unquestionably allowed ideas and cultures to flourish that otherwise would have never have emerged by allowing individual speakers to distance themselves from reprisals.

Early adopters of the internet years ago saw the anonymity as a key feature to the internet's value.

That said, the vast majority of people implicitly treat the anonymity of the internet as a bug. Certain governments, such as China, have made that decision at a macro level. Other communities have more implicitly chosen to recognize anonymity as a bug, opting for the convenience and value of having real identity as consumers and communicators on things like Amazon, Facebook, and Google's platforms. Strong online identity is critical to digital commerce, and is what allows us to trust the messages we read from friends.

In a post-Sept. 11 environment, most people got comfortable with giving up some degree of anonymity and privacy in return for security. In a post-Trump election environment, it is likely that we will be asked, and acquiesce, to giving up our ability to be someone else or speak in another voice online.

In most ways this could return us to the historical norm, where you generally are free to say what you will, but you were accountable for what you say. But it is unquestionable that this is a tectonic shift and will cause some people who used to feel free to speak to stop contributing their ideas and viewpoints.

Accountability will unquestionably limit some forms of speech, but it will also make the internet a far safer place. As a society, which endpoint do we prefer, one where we give back the internet's special property or one where we tolerate its implications?

2. Should Anyone Be Able to Reach Everyone?

If anonymity was the first magical property of the early internet, the second early property was that any individual could, at least in theory, reach anyone—or everyone—else.

Over the years this concept of total reach has evolved in fascinating ways. On one hand, in a practical sense, more individuals have more reach than ever before. The reach of scores of micro-celebrities in various niches has ballooned, giving individuals more power than they have ever held relative to institutions and formal gatekeepers.

This has led to a lot of good. For instance, the direct social media reach of individual celebrities is precisely what is allowing so much of the sexual misbehavior by powerful gatekeepers in Hollywood to be exposed.

And it isn't just celebrities. Social platforms in particular have made it easier for almost any individual to consistently communicate with and influence more people than ever before.

At the same time, at a technical level, the internet has grown in a direction of taking power away from others in non-obvious ways. The decline in the use of the open web in favor of social media and messaging means that people can't express themselves as they want in any way people will ever see. Instead, they have to conform to platform standards, be they iOS or social platforms or video hosting, if they want to have their content seen.

Even email, in theory still an open protocol, has been so severely locked down by providers, ostensibly to block spam, that it no longer is an open platform. Instead, you have to comply with several layers of gatekeepers if you ever want your messages delivered.

The upshot is that the debate is still very much open about who has access to mass distribution and on what terms individuals are allowed to speak to wider audiences.

If we decide that anyone should be able to reach everyone, then we need to be willing to tolerate a lot of painful speech. If we decide that that should no longer be the case as we chip away at the means of open distribution, who gets access to it, and the messages that are permissible, then we have to accept preventing some voices from expressing themselves broadly.

3. Is Money a Form of Speech?

If we decide that anyone should be able to reach everyone, then we need to be willing to tolerate a lot of painful speech.

While this question far predates the internet, digital communication has amplified it. Should I be free to spend money as an individual or institution to advocate for an idea I believe in? How do you regulate this?

Our laws in this area are murky. Spending money to endorse a candidate is governed by certain rules, but spending money to increase one's personal reach, fame and acclaim and then using non-paid scaled speech to endorse someone is acceptable.

Not all ideas cost the same to express. Because of dynamic pricing and targeting, where things that are more interesting or engaging are fundamentally less expensive to distribute online, there is a tendency for more extreme messages to be cheaper to distribute. So, we might have campaign finance laws and other rules about how much money a candidate can spend, but if one candidate's extremist message is 20 times less expensive to distribute than another candidate's centrist views, then the playing field is fundamentally unfair to moderates compared with an earlier world where all ad rates were the same for the same reach on TV and in print.

We could decide that money is a form of free speech and lift many of the murky rules on how money can be spent on distributing ideas. We also could decide to level the playing field on how money can be spent to distribute speech. What we shouldn't do is tolerate the current reality that we exist in, where arbitrage opportunities abound to use money in speech in unequal ways, fueling a bias toward ever more extreme statements.

4. Who Decides What Algorithms and Human Policies Control Our View of Reality?

Big platforms, faced with this enormous challenge while trying to avoid outside regulation, have consistently made the decision to bias toward building algorithms that attempt to prioritize or balance speech and add human moderation to deal with speech's fundamental messiness.

On one hand, they basically are forced to do this. Because they are centralized corporations with shareholders and employees, they have no option but to take on the increasingly serious and clearly Sisyphean task to decide what they will and won't allow to happen on their sites.

On the other hand, in doing this, private companies are effectively taking on a role in moderation of conversations that is unprecedented in human history, especially by a non-governmental organization.

This is uncomfortable, to say the least.

The global patchwork of jurisdictions, where large, multinational companies and hundreds of small and medium-size countries try to understand and control what speech is expressed is going to lead to some very strange and uncomfortable outcomes if this isn't clarified.

One option would be global government where the people, in some process, decide the ground rules we want to live by and then enforce the human and algorithmic application of those rules, and private companies stay completely out of the business of moderation.

Another option would be for governments to step back and let private platforms play the moderation role, choosing which algorithms and moderation tactics they think are best and then letting individuals choose which platforms they want to use.

A final option would be no moderation whatsoever, a scenario that we have been able to mostly maintain until now, but which is clearly beginning to crumble.

In all likelihood, we will choose none of these options and instead grapple with overlapping viewpoints and regulations globally. Such an outcome will either fracture the internet into local players aligned with local governments, or reach a point where only a small number of internet companies survive because it costs billions upon billions of dollars to navigate a fundamentally complicated global political landscape.

5. Will We Tolerate Unregulated Escape Hatches for Free Speech?

For a generation, the idea that communications technology has shrunk the world into a global village has been seen as a largely positive development in the technology community.

What is scary is that it is starting to feel that the collapse of the world into a pinhead online might actually be the first step in a chain reaction that, just like a nuclear weapon, will cause the world to violently explode. There is simply too much energy packed into too little space to be stable.

Historically, we have always had spaces for blowing off steam and preventing pressure from bubbling over. In the back rooms of pubs, at private parties in private homes, and in countless other unmonitored, safe spaces, individuals could speak their mind freely, out of the public eye.

But if the consolidation of the platforms of speech, power, and regulation persists, those spaces will evaporate and pressure will only build.

For now, none of the discussions about moderation of online communities has reached into private chat and speech. But it is only a matter of time before more private spaces come under scrutiny.

Don't Envy the Leaders

Philosophers have been debating questions similar to these for generations. What is pretty clear, however, is that the era of the primacy of John Stuart Mill and the Harm Principle has ended. What we do and say in any forum has real impact on others, which means we all have a stake in everything everyone else is doing.

The internet is forcing us to come up with new philosophical underpinnings for how we interact with each other. Realistically, whatever we come up with will make us sacrifice some priorities to achieve other goals.

No one is really equipped to deal with this shift. There is no script, and the reality is that no leader even has enough clout or jurisdiction to take the necessary steps. The exception here is perhaps China, whose model, while rejected by most in the West, at least seems to be a self-consistent way to manage a society.

The best we can hope for is that we actually make some hard decisions in the coming years rather than simply kicking the can down the road.

If we have a clear system with clear decisions about what we value and what we are willing to sacrifice, we will be able to move forward.

If, however, the result of the discussions about speech is continuous compromise and reactionary moves that try to thread the needle without taking on hard structural decisions, I fear we will end up a fractured civilization, unable to clearly hear or understand each other at a time when it is critical for us to be able to do both.

8: Blockchains and the Right to Be Forgotten

December 17, 2017

In the internet of 2017, when something goes terribly wrong, the service provider hosting the content or code can usually turn it off. But the rise of blockchains means that won't be the case for much longer.

One of the most interesting things about blockchains and the global computer superstructure being constructed on top of them is that blockchains can't forget—unlike the internet services of today. And code running on top of blockchains is nearly impossible to turn off.

THE TAKEAWAY
Blockchain technology challenges existing regulations governing content on the internet, rendering impractical the 'right to be forgotten' in Europe.

This shift—from today's internet technology to blockchain-based networks of the future—poses some particular challenges for regulators. We have already seen regulators struggle to deal with the implications of encrypted messaging. Soon, blockchains, which are built on cryptographic technology similar to that used in encrypted messaging, will pose even bigger challenges.

A generation ago, there were massive debates about the freedom of the internet. The largely free internet that happily emerged from those debates has, I believe, been a massive net positive (if at times challenging) thing for the world. In the next few years, those debates will happen all over again at even greater stakes, thanks to blockchains.

Permanent Distributed Memory vs. the Right to Be Forgotten

For many, the most powerful conceptualization of blockchain technology is that, if the technology is broadly enough distributed, it is impossible for the historical records kept in the blockchain to be erased or changed.

This is a core piece of why bitcoin and its brethren are so appealing to those who worry about the concentration of power in the modern world. Bitcoin is the embodiment of a form of value and a medium of transaction that powerful organizations can't censor or freeze.

That logic, of a distributed ledger, can be extended far beyond a simple record of accounts. Anything you could store in a database you could, in theory, store on a blockchain—text, photos, video, etc. Putting it on a blockchain, while perhaps somewhat inefficient, would make it impossible to remove or reverse.

To understand what this means in a practical sense, consider the European concept of the "right to be forgotten."

The idea behind the right to be forgotten is that a person can require service providers like search engines and social networks to remove content about them. The spirit of the law is that you should own the information about you.

This law has always been inane in my mind for one practical and one philosophical reason. The practical reason is that because it is basically impossible to audit whether "your" content is gone or not, it is basically impossible to enforce—and rules that can't be enforced are generally bad rules.

Philosophically, the right to be forgotten is corrupt because it basically assaults a person or a company's right to remember things. There have been countless heated arguments throughout history about the right of free speech, but almost no one in history has ever argued about my right to remember things. It was impractical—except in the movie "Men In Black"— to even discuss a person or organization's right to its own memory. But, the right to remember—if questioned—is perhaps the most important right we have as a species. It is what gives us the ability to have a society where we build relationships and trust one another.

The blockchain, by its very construct, removes all questions about the right to remember. The entire technology relies upon the fact that no data, once written, can be removed from the blockchain. That is its value.

What does this mean for Europe's right to be forgotten? In a world of blockchains, it is literally an impossible law. The technology dictates that people have about as much a right to be forgotten as they do to fly—it is impossible.

More broadly, the blockchain undercuts any laws we (or service providers) have had barring certain content on the internet—from nipples to defamation. Once that content has been published, it can't be removed.

That is the massive opportunity and a challenge. The prospect that people can collaborate to generate new forms of global trust without relying on central organizations is particularly relevant today, when trust in ISPs is diminishing. And it is also a very challenging concept for the traditional systems of power that currently exist.

Philosophically, the right to be forgotten is corrupt because it basically assaults a person or a company's right to remember things.

Unstoppable Computer Systems; Enabling the Next Silk Road, Rogue AIs and Resilient Infrastructure

If the blockchains by their nature make removing content from the internet impossible, they also effectively make code that runs on top of blockchains impossible to stop once it is released.

Just like unstoppable memory, unstoppable computer code is something that many people see as important to the future of freedom and a casus belli—something worth fighting for.

It is easy to see why. In a world that feels ever more centralized and fraught with controversy, building guarantees that important platforms or systems can't be easily shut off seems very important. After all, it was a desire for distribution in light of the nuclear war threat that contributed to the invention of the internet in the first place.

There is, however, some difficult implications to systems like this that are worth acknowledging. Take, for instance, the case of the Silk Road and Silk Road 2. These websites were difficult for governments to shut down—but they succeeded eventually.

At some point, however, someone is going to build a version of Silk Road that sits on top of some blockchain—and that one will be much much harder (even potentially impossible) to turn off. Once the code is there and any sort of brand or community is built, these systems will be extremely resilient to any attempt to turn them off.

Even beyond that, consider the worries some people have about rogue AI-based systems. In today's world, I believe most people who worry about unstoppable rogue AI are being alarmist—because we can always unplug it. But, in a blockchain-based world, that might no longer be so easy.

This is the nature of blockchain technology. It is a tool that has both very positive and usually very scary implications. Good and bad will come of it.

The Balance of Knowledge-Power

I consider myself both an optimist and a technological determinist. I believe that now that blockchains exist as a technology, they will be built, improved and used.

I believe that they will bring massive good and stability to the world, creating a framework where we can not only trust speech, but create a truly safe space for collective memory. The first use case might be digital gold—giving broad access to an "inflation proof" way to store value away from local market manipulation. But the long-term use cases for such a system go far, far beyond what we currently see.

That said, this next internet revolution is going to be—in time—as disruptive, if not more so, than the first internet revolution. Technology is going to force laws and social mores to change. And, like many periods of radical growth and change, it is going to be a painful and disruptive transition.

9: Open vs. Closed in National Tech Strategies: the U.S. and China

January 29, 2018

In the last several months, the Chinese government has moved swiftly to manage and shape self-driving cars, genetics data and cryptocurrencies in their country—arguably the three most promising technologies of the immediate future.

The Chinese are very good at this managed-closed strategy. Their top-down approach has some clear benefits over more open models for innovation and technology. And it poses a clear choice for a comparatively small country like the United States.

THE TAKEAWAY
The U.S. should centralize policy making in some key areas, like self-driving cars, but adopt a more open approach around capital raising. We don't have the scale to succeed at the fully-closed strategy pursued by the Chinese.

We can choose to go toward a more closed model, or we can go in the completely opposite direction and open up everything. Does the United States want to be a second-rate walled garden, or go open-source with all the messiness that will certainly follow? The question is a timely one given news reports over the weekend that the Trump administration has <u>considered nationalizing</u> the 5G network.

The Option to Close Up

China's approach means it will have:

- The largest genetics and health data sets in the world with which to push forward innovation, and they will keep it for themselves.

- Faster paths for domestic automakers to release self-driving cars and harvest the efficiencies from increased logistical capabilities.

- Firm control over domestic economic policy and how assets are owned and transferred, by controlling how blockchain technologies are used.
We could have the same. In theory, we could choose to adopt the same top-down closed model that the Chinese have chosen for the next generation of technology. We could attempt to weaken the states and strengthen national technology oversight and control.

But the reality is that this strategy is likely to fail us on a global scale even if it were politically viable, which it clearly isn't in our democracy.

We are entering an era of return on scale, and we just don't have the scale.

In the case of genetics, the value of incremental data probably peaks at some point once you have enough data. But that number is pretty clearly not 300 million people.

The same goes with transportation infrastructure. Setting aside the fact that our infrastructure is far older and less standardized, our market is big—but not big enough. The one billion-plus number of Chinese people looking to move around efficiently in scores of megalopolises are going to drive innovation far faster with red-tape cleared, than our small and less dense population will.

So, we could choose the same model as the Chinese, and move toward a more closed version of innovation. But we will not be as competitive as they are.

The Completely Open Path

What if we aggressively took the opposite approach, and decided to become very, very open as a country? This would mean opening borders and data sets fully, deregulating and even encouraging genetics experimentation and letting anything on the road that anyone wants to drive. It would mean sharing openly all the data we have and allowing an open flourishing of crypto-assets, tokenizations and offerings. It would mean letting new local communities and small governments form within the country with little or no oversight of the state.

The rose-tinted picture of this would be some sort of return to the glorified West of the 1800s. Lots of opportunity, almost no rules or oversight, innovators and inventors having free reign to develop and collaborate and test as they see fit. And by collaborating with the entire world, it would also mean opportunities for generating more scale than we have as a nation alone.

I don't think any society can function at any scale with a fully open strategy, as much as many West Coast technologists would like to believe it possible.

The less optimistic reality of such a move would probably also have a lot in common with the deregulated "free zones" of science fiction. It would be dangerous, unsupported, polluted, extremely unequal and, at times, very scary.

Open borders—which would undoubtedly allow for an influx of talent and opportunity— would almost certainly mean massively curtailed social services.

Open finance and securitization would mean far easier access to capital, but also scams and volatility galore.

Light or no regulation of data policies and genetics would lead to some seriously unequal and unfair outcomes—and in the case of genetics some very dangerous ones.

Open or Closed

So, assuming we had the political will to choose, what would you choose?

All open or all closed is probably a big mistake. In an era of super-empowered individuals and technology, the all open model is too unstable and dangerous. But, simultaneously, being a small closed kingdom in the era of extreme and immediate return on scale is a poor position to be in.

The solution in my mind should be picking a few key verticals or places where you want to be aggressively open, and then a few key places where taking a closed stance is the best. But don't confuse the two.

That would mean, for instance, centralizing the DMV and giving control over deployment of self-driving technology to one entity as a closed choice. But it would also mean dramatically simplifying the rules around capital raising and tokenization as an open choice in another space.

I don't think any society can function at any scale with a fully open strategy, as much as many West Coast technologists would like to believe it possible.

But I do think that the most important choice we can make right now is clarity on what our strategy is and then logically following through, versus the patchwork of open and closed sub-scale strategies we currently use.

10: The Intellectual Tension Between Social Networking and Blockchains

Feb 12, 2018

There is an interesting irony that social networks and blockchains, two of the most important information technologies of the day, sit in fundamental intellectual tension.

The core idea of a blockchain is that there is a common shared "memory" on which all nodes choose to agree. In a blockchain-based world, consensus is both the goal and the value. If you as an individual choose to disagree with the majority, you are an outcast and thrown out of the system.

THE TAKEAWAY
Usually we think of centralization and consistency going hand in hand. The same holds true of decentralization and nuance. But blockchains and social networks may be reversing those historical norms.

The idea of a social network, in contrast, is that there is no central point of truth. Instead, all information and claims are a matter of perspective based on who you listen to in a network. The network itself—in the abstract—has no "opinion" but simply serves as a medium through which each participant can construct their own viewpoint.

That social network "relativist" view of the world is today considered deeply challenging. And many people see in blockchains the exciting potential to build the consistent shared digital memory that is considered critical for well-functioning global societies of the near future.

But I wonder if this is a case of the grass being greener on the other side.

If blockchain technology had been invented and deployed before social networking existed, would we be in the opposite position—decrying the forced consistency and lack of nuance of blockchain-based truth and yearning for the unfettered relativity of gossip and perspective afforded by social networks?

The reality is that neither social networks nor the blockchain model for information is complete on its own.

Blockchains are slow, highly inefficient and will never be able to handle nuance by fundamental design. That's because in order for information to exist in a blockchain context, there needs to be many copies of that "reality" redundantly spread around the world.

Running something like Facebook on top of a blockchain architecture would be somewhere between silly and impossible. It would be a massive waste of resources and time to secure the integrity of every comment, like, photo and post through the process of distribution and consensus.

On the other hand, social networks are incapable of generating the same degree of trust that blockchains can. They can accommodate incredible nuance and a diversity of opinions efficiently. But the cost of that nuance is that you have to give control of "memory" over to a centralized node, which will never be fully trusted no matter how well intentioned.

There is some degree of irony to the relationship between these two technologies.

Historically, we think of centralization and consistency going hand in hand. The same holds true for decentralization and nuance.

If blockchain technology had been invented and deployed before social networking existed, would we be in the opposite position—decrying the forced consistency and lack of nuance of blockchain-based truth?

That is how things work in the physical world. Centralized governments and institutions kept the key final records of account, but decentralized town squares held all the nuance of perspective and knowledge.

But with blockchains and social networks, we might be seeing the opposite.

Centralized social networking services are efficient enough to be able to accommodate tons of nuance and perspective. Blockchains are decentralized in storage but, in their decentralization, tend to force consistency and agreement.

As we continue to cycle between centralization and decentralization, on one hand, and a desire for consensus about facts versus more contextual nuance on another, a strange flip is occurring. Decentralization is now paired with consistency, and centralization with nuance.

For the first time, centralization is the key to nuance, and decentralization is the safe harbor for consistency—instead of the other way around.

Ultimately, for a vibrant future, we need both technologies.

We need both an ever-more vibrant and expansive public square. We also need more trustworthy and agreed-upon records of globally shared context.

Asking either technology to do the work of the other is highly undesirable.

As I have suggested <u>before</u>, I believe in a hybrid future involving decentralized systems when trust is most critical and centralization for systems where efficiency is more important than trust.

The key is to understand that each technology is suitable to its own type of content. What we should choose to centralize or decentralize in the future virtual world is actually inverted from what we would have chosen a century ago.

11: Governing the Internet

April 9, 2018

It has always been inevitable that regulation would come to the internet just as it has come to every major communications platform that preceded it. Once the Web became critical infrastructure and started down the path of consolidation to just a handful of large platforms, it was only a matter of time.

What is less clear is exactly what the regulation that comes should look like and how much the platforms will be trusted to self regulate rather than needing an outsider to set rules. Here are the most important points to keep in mind as technology and government parley over the coming months.

THE TAKEAWAY
Technology has given us the ability for the first time to police nuanced issues around speech and information. We have abdicated decision-making to the big technology platforms, which are in an unwinnable position—forced to try to resolve big, complicated social questions. How do we move forward from here?

Consolidation and machine learning have opened a Pandora's box on a host of historically unimaginable speech and memory issues that society is ill-equipped to address.

It is easy for Americans to agree that freedom of speech is broadly good. There are, however, an enormous number of nuanced issues surrounding speech, information and ownership about which there is little understanding and less agreement.

How do we value information freedom versus information security? What rights do others have over my right to self expression? If I say something, who has the right to repeat it and in what ways? What rights do I have to my own memory if that memory includes other people? Who owns data or insights derived partially from "my" data and mixed with data provided by others? In a world where I used tools to generate content, what rights can the tools claim? What liability is involved in not catching signals from speech that could save lives? What is unacceptable speech? What rights do people have versus the state to private communication? What can and can't people agree to? How sacred is contract law in dealings between people and companies?

The list goes on and on, and where once these were all academic we now have the technology, tools, and consolidation to police and therefore regulate speech at this level.

We see this all around us today.

A seemingly tiny question like whether or not Mark Zuckerberg should be allowed to "un-send" messages sent over Facebook Messenger is just a taste of an enormous issues with deep social impact—what rights do people have to "take back" digitally shared content, and how does that trade against a person's rights to remember conversations?

A seemingly good idea like <u>allowing people to upload images of their bodies</u> to help platforms block the sharing of "revenge porn" unlocks a tool for moderation that will almost certainly then be stretched to more challenging uses.

The question of whether you as a user of a platform should be allowed to take your 'data' beyond the walls of one service to another may seem reasonably easy to decide. At least, until you get into the details of how exactly you define "your" data versus that of others and information derived from "your" data.

Then there is the even bigger issue of contract law. How sacred is it? The Europeans have decided that there are some terms of service that consumers don't have the freedom as individuals to agree to. Do we want to go down that fundamentally un-American path?

We now enjoy new technological superpowers. But as a society, we have to decide how we want those powers used. And we come from a place where almost no one is informed enough to debate these deep issues, let alone come to sensible agreement.

Because we can't agree as a society on how to handle these issues, we have abdicated decision making to technology platforms. They can't possibly satisfy all parties in the U.S., let alone globally, and are set up to fail.

On one level I feel for the leadership teams at technology companies who have been left to try to sort out these issues on their own. They are in an unwinnable position.

Every affirmative policy or decision they try to enact about fundamental speech, safety or freedom comes with massive loss and liability and will enrage a large group of people who disagree with the implications.

Americans as a group couldn't agree on these rules—how could a global population? And I strongly believe that the issues are far too complicated for our representative democracy to sort out, especially in this era. And so we leave the decisions to the private sector, knowing full well that any decision they make will be seen by a large group of people as both very important and fundamentally wrong.

Just a few years ago a large chorus agitated for data openness, fearing Facebook's powerful walled garden. A few years later the small steps that were made toward that end are ridiculed as unsafe.

It feels like game of rule hot potato. The leaders are set up to fail.

Compounding their unwinnable position, the technology platforms have tried to placate all parties and in the process created overly complicated and nearly incomprehensible set of rules

On Friday, Jessica wrote an excellent column about how technology companies made a big policy attempt to be loved rather than trusted. I couldn't agree more, and I think you can see the hallmarks of this not just in their PR strategy but also in product decisions.

Big platforms have attempted to placate all parties over these maddeningly complex issues by adding more rules, conditions, monitoring and settings— instead of taking simple and trustable "stands" on key issues.

Their desire to placate regulators, be 'liked' by users, and have an answer for each discrete issue or question as it comes up leads to a conflicted and inconsistent overall system.

If you are willing to be disliked by some, you can build logical models that people could choose to use.

If we decide to take decision-making power on these issues out of the hands of the technology platforms and come up with formal laws we will likely squash innovation and cement the power of the existing companies

It should be lost on no one that the regulation of big internet companies would in many ways be an enormous gift to the incumbents.

History tells us that this is what regulatory capture looks like. Big companies run up against big issues, the government steps in, and rules get created that the biggest existing players can afford to live by—but which startups cannot.

This most recently happened around hedge funds. The chorus from fund managers went quickly from "please don't regulate us" to "we need regulation." And since that time the big funds have been cemented in place, able to afford the accounting and compliance costs. Meanwhile, it has become much harder and more expensive to start a fund.

Let's pretend that for the sake of security the government decides to force platforms to adopt banking-like KYC standards—where to sign up and serve someone you must have state and federal IDs, and reams of paperwork.

Apple, Google, and Facebook might not like this. It will cost them users and also disenfranchise all sorts of populations like illegal immigrants who they might want to serve. But they have the business models and reach to comply (Facebook in fact just in the last few days volunteered that they would do this for pages and advertisers). Startups don't have those luxuries.

What will happen? Fewer startups? New business for the big companies validating identities for startups? The results are hard to predict, but it is clear that a law like this will only help the existing winners.

If you worry today that big companies have too much of an advantage on key next-generation technology like AI because of the scale of their data sets, just wait until regulation makes it dramatically harder for the next data-sets to be built.

Any regulation that gets passed down needs to be comprehensible, simple, enforceable and self-consistent—which is a challenging if not impossible equilibrium to maintain

Just because this is all very complicated doesn't mean I don't think we should do anything.

On one level I feel for the leadership teams at technology companies who have been left to try to sort out these issues on their own. They are in an unwinnable position.

Over a year ago, right after President Trump won the election, I proposed <u>in a column</u> that Facebook needed to make an open and searchable database of all the ads run on its platform along with its targeting criteria so that watchdog organizations could understand what messages were being delivered to people. About 10 months later, Facebook announced that they would do just that.

Requiring this would be a good law that perhaps should be passed at a national level. If you pay money to deliver a message to other people, what the message said and who you said it to should be public record. The law is easy to write and understand, easy to comply with, and highly enforceable. It might ever so slightly advantage incumbents who didn't need to abide by the rule on their way up, and who can afford the extra reporting requirements. But the burden is small and the advantages are clear.

What I worry about, however, is more of the GDPR-style regulations that have a host of opposite problems—creating regulatory frameworks that are hard to monitor and enforce, and have potentially very strange outcomes for not just technology but how we think about memory and speech.

Oversight into algorithms, controls around what people can or can't say or remember, content blockage or removal, and murky morals guidelines are tempting trees to bark up. But when you get down to the details of how things like this would be encoded and regulated, the tendency is toward rules which are hard or impossible to understand and enforce at scale.

Further, any rules set in stone will have negative consequences for some. For example, KYC regulations will undeniably disenfranchise people. The tendency of laws will be to balloon and become increasingly conditional and complex as elected officials look to solve for distasteful corner cases— like the privacy frameworks for large technology platforms have to date. This will end in disaster.

Any regulation that gets passed needs to be forward compatible with new technology on the horizon, and acknowledge that the U.S. is at best a regional player in a global game—both of which are hard pills to swallow

We are a small part of the world's population. The technology of the internet today isn't fixed and will keep evolving. If new rules make our internet companies globally uncompetitive then the U.S. will not be the place that global technology platforms are based.

Even more challengingly, if rules are set that make the current framework of centralized services less competitive, then decentralized systems, blockchain-based solutions, etc. will just grow more quickly. And they are far harder to regulate (if even possible).

There are already cracks in the internet as a global force. China has largely opted out of the global internet and Europe has made moves in its own direction, if less radically. What about us and the rest of the world?

I certainly believe a few well-constructed rules that apply only to Americans and American politics could work. But I fear that moves we make—tipping our hat toward closing down our open internet borders just as the current administration is backing away from global free trade—could rapidly devolve into a full fracturing of the internet on national lines.

This would be a tragedy in my mind, and lead to a net loss of American reach and power in the word.

Crypto as a Template for Defensive Design

So, contemplating all of these challenges, what can we do to move forward? How should platforms self-regulate, and what types of rules could governments look to enforce?

After a long period of Silicon Valley over-optimism, I think we as a culture need to embrace defensive system design, with a clear understanding of what rules become natively enforceable and what things aren't possible to control.

We can't rely upon concepts like "best efforts" in a globalized world. We can't rely upon paper contracts and agreements that live outside of code to save us.

Instead, we need to bake the core principles of what we believe and how systems should work deeply into the technology itself, and acknowledge that where we can't encode the rules directly into the system we probably can't reasonably regulate—or where the cost of regulation fundamentally alters the system itself.

Cryptocurrencies in general, and bitcoin in particular, are a good recent example of how this can be done. The crypto ecosystem starts with the belief that their systems will constantly be under assault by sophisticated actors, and all exploits that can be tried will be tried. This limits crypto, but it also makes it fundamentally powerful, and makes the developers of crypto products focus intently on the extreme cases that will "break" their systems.

We can't make regulations that, for instance, limit the data that people or systems choose to remember or store. Those types of regulations—while possibly emotionally appealing in some cases—are fundamentally unenforceable.

For the same reason, we also can't write laws that sandbox data, saying that it can only be used by certain actors for certain purposes. Once data exists, it is extremely hard to control where it goes, whose hands it ends up in, and what it is used for.

What we can do is build defensive technical systems that don't leak data by accident, and add regulation that works at the interface between technical systems and real world goods like attention and money. I can contemplate rules that force transparency in paid speech, limit the distribution (but don't ban) anonymous speech, and give consumers insight into what companies know about them. These all seems like potential wins.

But in the end, my hope is that regardless of whether we end up with formal regulation or more self-regulation we center on very simple and unambiguously enforceable rules. If a third grader can't learn and understand it, we have done it wrong.

Facebook is an easy target, but the company isn't really the main event. The real issue is that our core identity and digital infrastructure is antiquated

This week Mark Zuckerberg will be in Washington to take a public lashing from senators as the most visible representative of the technology industry facing these challenges.

It make sense.

Facebook is the biggest brand associated in people's minds with these challenging questions and has been out front for a host of reasons, including an obviously strained relationship with the press, which has forgotten its once-fraught relationship with Google in the early days of the web.

But it is worth remembering in all this that while Facebook is an easy target, it is by no means the most complicated case in the question of data ownership, security and the regulation of bits.

The far more challenging cases are those that collect massive data sets without consumers knowing and in non-transparent ways. That includes the ISPs, the Equifaxes and the finance companies that build massive treasure troves of consumer data without direct relationships with their customers, clear terms of service, and records of what they know and how they share it.

The real issue is that our core societal technology for identity, security, privacy, and data management based around old, simple, and completely unsophisticated technologies like social security numbers and addresses has been totally outclassed by new digital technology. Overhauling these core systems is what really should be on trial.

This conversation may open with Facebook on the Hill, but it will not by any means close with it.

12: It's Time for an American Internet Privacy Framework

June 19, 2018

In the last several weeks, you likely received a slew of emails from U.S. internet companies updating privacy policies in response to the Europe's General Data Protection Regulation privacy rules coming into effect.

Seeing these updates has left me with a nagging question: Why are all these U.S.-domiciled companies choosing to update their services to comply with laws that might not even apply to them from a jurisdictional perspective?

THE TAKEAWAY
The U.S. needs to establish its own version of internet data law, rather than allow Europe to become America's de facto regulator through a strange quirk of history.

The seemingly obvious answer is that with global reach—or at least global ambitions—most of these companies feel compelled to default to the globally lowest common denominator—the most restrictive terms—when it comes to following data regulation.

But what is going on is actually far more complicated, and frankly more problematic.

Trust in American internet companies is at a low point, and the most complete answer to why they are choosing to comply with GDPR is that there is no competing U.S. framework for companies to stand behind.

This wouldn't necessarily be a bad thing if the GDPR framework were a good set of laws; however, I worry that many of the ideas that underpin the framework are extremely dangerous to the long-term health and security of democracy, and against American ideals.

It would have been nice if the internet had been able to stay free and open, but as it has become more powerful, it was only a matter of time before regulation started to come into play.

The reality is that if we need to deal with a fractured and regionalized internet, the U.S. needs to assert a version of internet data law, rather than allow the Europeans to become America's de facto regulator through a strange quirk of history.

Why The U.S. Shouldn't Accept the European Way of Privacy

Creating a competing U.S. privacy framework wouldn't perhaps be so pressing if the GDPR represented a set of good regulations. But sadly, there are several deeply questionable elements of the European regulation. Here are four of the key issues:

1. Bad Laws

First among the challenges with the GDPR is that it contains some simply bad laws. Chief among the bad ideas is the "Right to Be Forgotten."

The right to remember is, in many ways, even more fundamental than the right to free speech. I should have a fundamental right to save and use the correspondence, photos and data to which I have been granted access, just as I have the right to remember anything I have seen or learned in the real world. The only reason that the right to free memory isn't in the Constitution is that it would have never occurred to the Founding Fathers that the right to memory was a possibly practical issue.

The European way implies that I as an individual have some sort of ownership or claim over all the information about me in the world.

This isn't how reality works. We interact with other people and businesses who build memories, opinions and perspectives about us, and who use that to make informed decisions about how they would like to interact with us in the future.

Even beyond philosophy it is worth considering the human side of memory. Most of my memories of myself are rooted in conversations and interactions with others. It is impossible for me as an individual to "forget" someone else without simultaneously losing a part of myself.

Thus, the right to remember, or the right to memory, is perhaps the most deeply critical human right if you want to have a functioning society where we can trust and interact with each other well over time.

I respect and understand how Europeans came to believe in something like the Right to Be Forgotten. In Europe, the memory of the Holocaust is strong and visceral, and it seems to lead people to a different place in terms of things like Freedom of Speech and Freedom of Memory.

But their approach isn't in keeping with the American perspective.

I am convinced that the Right to Be Forgotten, along with related GDPR articles including the Right to Rectification (based on whose truth?), and Right to Data Portability (define "your" data?) are going to be very dangerous when you look at a historical scale.

2. Unenforceability

The second among many challenges with GDPR is that it is impossible to enforce technically. Take, for instance, blockchain technologies. As I have written about before, they are fundamentally incompatible with GDPR. The whole idea of a blockchain is that it is a platform for permanent irrevocable memory. When you contrast that with a legal regime that asks for data to be delete-able, you quickly reach an impasse.

This isn't just a future-looking issue. There also are massive issues with GDPR in terms of how auditing and enforcement can work today.

When you make assertions about what I can and can't store on a hard drive or remember, you have to be able to then validate what I as an individual or service do or don't know. Those types of requirements pose interesting questions about what powers we want to give over to governments to monitor our activities and our privacy from the government.

I would argue that the implications of GDPR run up against American concepts like the Fourth Amendment, which prohibits unreasonable searches and seizures.

3. Complexity

The third issue I would call out about the GDPR is simply its complexity. The regulation alone is 88 pages. The interpretations by various parties run orders of magnitude longer.

To deal with all the complexity, ironically, data services are already cropping up to mediate between data warehouses and end-user services, allowing the end-user services to comply with GDPR by offloading the legal and policy complexity of warehousing data to other firms.

So, there is a world where, ironically, what GDPR actually ends up doing is empowering certain data custodians and warehouses more, not less, as firms that used to manage data on their own are forced to outsource to third parties for compliance reasons.

Good laws are simple laws that are meaningful and enforceable. With GDPR, we instead have a series of weak and confusing guidelines that will be hard for any company to reasonably keep up with from a principles-first perspective.

4. Regulatory Capture and Competitive Calcification

It should be lost on no one that GDPR is great for the large internet companies. They are best able to comply and have had open regulations and road to grow on for years, if not decades.

In fact, it has been quite interesting to watch companies like Apple and Facebook taking this moment and using it to further extend how they limit and lock down data in and around their platforms. Apple changed its terms of service to prevent many scenarios in which user data used to be central to how developers used their APIs. Facebook just added new agreements around the use of custom audiences. This is all happening as the companies look to build on the moment to their advantage.

Throwing up new barriers and making managing user data more expensive and harder simply entrenches large internet companies more and makes it harder for newer companies to compete.

So, ironically, GDPR makes data that providers already have used more valuable.

This is classic regulatory capture. As with environmental discussions in which smaller countries like to point out how many years the now-developed world had free rein to pollute the world as they grew, only to now block developing nations from following the same course, GDPR entrenches large internet companies and makes life more difficult for the next player coming up.

The American Way

Of course, it is easy to criticize other people's law or rules, and far more difficult to come up with better counter-proposals. That said, let me try to outline a few things I think could underpin a U.S. privacy framework.

1. The Right to Remember

All individuals and companies should have the right to remember their interactions with others and their history.

There is an argument that, in the digital age, the right to remember needs to be further enforced than it once was, granting extra protection to individuals over their private photos, videos and writing. That might mean personal papers should get new levels of freedom and protection, so that they couldn't be used to incriminate their authors, for example, in a world where everything is written down and recorded.

Your personal records—which are extensions of your own mind—should be your property, and they shouldn't be able to be used against you.

2. The Right to Know Your Audience

In the real world, you say things in the context of physical and social spaces. We have as humans thousands of years of experience choosing what we want to say and how we want to present ourselves in different situations to different people.

One of the real challenges of the internet is that it is very difficult to think of it as a "space" and to think about whom you are speaking to and what spaces you are occupying when you post on a social network, fill out a form on a website, etc.

Many internet services have benefitted from this for a long time, making people feel comfortable broadcasting to large audiences from their homes in seemingly intimate digital spaces.

I think that internet service providers should be forced to tell users when they post to whom the post will be visible. It also is reasonable that web services should disclose in plain language what data they, and their agents, are collecting from you as you use their systems.

3. The Right to Message Delivery

One of the most innovative ideas during the formation of the U.S. government was the postal system. In order to foster a healthy society, the idea was developed that the post office would deliver a message from anyone to anyone else, and you could have complete faith that the transmission wouldn't be tampered with or halted.

This used to be the model of the internet as well. You couldn't stop an email from being delivered if sent, and clients could sort the mail they received into what they viewed as important and what they considered "junk."

Over the last 20 years, as the number of internet service providers has consolidated, that open nature of the web and messaging is evaporating. There are now layers of service providers sitting in the middle of all messaging mediums and deciding which messages to pass through and which to block.

This comes from a good place—an attempt to limit spam and scams. But the ability to block certain people from sending messages to other people leaves the world in a dangerous place.

A good internet framework should focus on the unimpeded transmission of messages, so that internet messaging can maintain the same fundamental trust as the U.S. Postal Service over the long term.

4. The Right to Anonymous Access

One of the most famous early internet cartoons was the New Yorker's iconic picture of dogs using the internet, where one dog says to the other, "On the internet, no one knows you're a dog."

This has dramatically changed over the last 20 years. Now, everyone not only knows what dog you are, but exactly which breed.

To protect privacy, we need a law in the U.S. that guarantees that you can sign up for any service using a simple username and password, versus being forced to choose a more data-rich login option like Google or Facebook open authorization.

This doesn't mean that the service needs to provide the same degree of access for users who haven't connected other services or are "less trusted" users in the system. It is clear that companies should be able to encourage or require certain types of validations or information in order to access certain features.

But services shouldn't be able to unduly discriminate against my usage if I refuse to log in with a data-rich profile. Any functionality that can be reasonably provided without connecting a third-party service should be accessible without that access.

5. The Right of Records of Agreements

When you use the internet, you agree to all sorts of terms and conditions. I propose we establish some sort of right to make sure these agreements are transparent and simple. Put simply, you have a right to know exactly what you signed.

You as a user should always have the right to all agreements you consent to in order to use the internet in an auditable way.

In practical terms, this would mean that with every agreement you click "OK" to or agree to in order to use a website, you should receive an email with the exact copy so that it can be audited at a later date.

6. The Right to One-Click Cancellation

As the world moves more toward subscription services, there is more of an incentive to make it difficult to try to unsubscribe from services you are paying for.

For instance, I dare you to try to figure out how to unsubscribe from the New York Times online.

At the extreme, some internet services even make you call a physical phone line to cancel their service and stop being billed. This is clearly bad.

I would be in favor of regulation requiring that you as an individual need to be able to unsubscribe from any service online in no more than three clicks, though one would be ideal. If you make it easy for me to pay, you need to make it easy for me to stop paying.

The Path Forward

At Fin, the AI-powered digital assistant company I co-founded, we for years have had in our terms of service that Europeans aren't allowed to register for our services, in anticipation of GDPR.

More recently, we have blocked European IP addresses, and made it clear in all communications that we only ever offer services in the U.S. to Americans.

We aren't alone in this approach. Several newspapers, retailers and other organizations have made the same decision. Europeans are now simply too high risk and too high complexity to serve.

Intellectually, I find it fascinating. I can't wait for an American company not operating in Europe but serving people in Europe to be fined, and for the world to have to sort out the associated jurisdictional issues (my bet is that the Europeans won't ever be able to collect).

Practically, I find it a bit sad. I wish we could keep the internet open, and I wish that Europe weren't cutting itself off from so much innovation.

Optimistically, I hope that this is the opening for the U.S. to outline a real set of rules and values for U.S. companies that would update and clarify some much-needed points of law for the digital age.

13: The Future of Privacy: Disinformation

August 20, 2018

Between 2007 and 2010, I lived in New York and worked on a startup called drop.io, whose goal was to make it easy to privately share files and content across platforms. Given what I was working on in that period, I spent a lot of time talking about privacy.

One theme—which I would highlight over and over in presentations—was that the only possible <u>future of privacy was to generate lots of disinformation</u> rather than try to prevent information from being exposed in the first place. In other words, bury the truth in a sea of lies.

THE TAKEAWAY
The strategically correct way to react to modern technology and protect privacy in 2018 is to share lots of disinformation, burying the truth in a sea of lies instead of trying to protect the truth itself. But there are fundamental flaws in this as a long-term approach.

It dawned on me last week that perhaps the greatest modern practitioner of this new form of privacy is Donald Trump. Perhaps because of his decades of public "celebrity" life, he seems to intuitively understand modern privacy better than almost everyone. He seems to really get that privacy isn't about hiding, it is about speaking constantly.

The key is not to try to prevent things from coming out. The key is to put out so much chaff along with the truth that it is impossible to know what is real and what is fake—and eventually everyone gives up trying to separate the two.

The New Yorker recently ran a column comparing a recent Trump admission—about meeting with Russians to learn about Hillary Clinton—to the Watergate "smoking gun" tape. But the column made the point that whereas Nixon admitted the meaning of what he was heard saying on the tape and that it would lead to his impeachment, Trump's alternative strategy is to try to bend reality.

Whether or not you agree with the New Yorker's example, there are other instances of the Trump strategy. For example, there is his recent meeting with Putin where he decided to say one thing on stage, and then days later have his team claim he meant to say the exact opposite.

That is what is so ironic about his claims that serious publications are "fake news." His core strategy is to himself generate enough fake news in other channels and then try to create an equivalence between all information sources.

It seems like, so far, this is a very successful strategy for the president—at least so far as his goals are purely privacy.

By being insanely active on Twitter and other channels, and—in effect—saying all things, whether contradictory or not, he simultaneously says nothing. And he is able to achieve his goal of keeping reality private—known only to himself.

As I was preaching 10 years ago, this is a strategy in general that we should all expect to see more and more in the world. It is, I would argue, the aggressively technologically correct strategy to run for the future. Don't prevent leaks or try to lock down everything. Just build self-serving networks of people or bots to put out enough false information to obscure reality.

If you are a private person, don't try to avoid having a social media profile. Instead try to have many fake ones, all sharing contradictory information about "you."

As technologically correct as this strategy will be in the short term for individuals and organizations looking to protect themselves, it has two really fundamental long-term flaws.

The first flaw is that it is broadly terrible for humanity overall. It is effectively pollution in our shared pool of knowledge and understanding of the world. Such is the tragedy of any commons. The individual incentive is to pollute, and over time the entire space becomes unusable.

I worry that that is precisely what is happening to our current public discourse. The commons is actively being polluted, so different groups are retreating to private spaces for real discussion.

The second flaw, which perhaps the president will care more about, is that it is very, very difficult to control. In traditional access-based privacy control models, the goal is to keep some people out but let other people "in" to know a fact.

The problem with the strategy of flooding the information zone is that it is very hard to keep certain people out and other people in. The strategy effectively requires you to be tricking and creating confusion for everyone, not just certain people.

So, the Faustian bargain of the disinformation game becomes that you can have privacy, but you have privacy from everyone—not just some people.

Just like the old simple tale of the boy who cried wolf, at some point the disinformation strategy means that your voice loses all meaning—and you lose the ability to communicate with others, even when you want to.

Some people like to pretend that no one saw this coming. But for what it's worth, I think many people understood that this was a logical step that would happen as the internet developed.

The question, of course, is what to do about it and how to fix it—and that will be my next column.

14: How the Internet Broke and What to Do About It

Sept 4, 2018

Any thinking person should realize that we face major challenges when it comes to the future of free speech and the internet. Disinformation and coordinated manipulation are a real, serious and unrelenting reality. Rightly and wrongly the claims of bias abound, and the broad lack of trust in what we read and see is palpable and growing.

For generations in the pre-internet physical world, we as a society balanced ideals of free speech with privacy, safety and security. But in the new frictionless digital environment, these ideologies are in fundamental and immediate tension in new ways.

THE TAKEAWAY
There are three possible ways to deal with the deep challenges of free speech on the internet. We will need to explicitly choose between giving near complete control of speech to the government, using new technology to guarantee complete freedom of speech or accepting permanent tension between governments, platforms and people.

More complicated still, <u>as I have written before</u>, we are also simultaneously living through the collapse of the distinction between the public and private spheres, making it hard to continue to draw historically clear policy lines between private speech in closed groups and messaging threads and public speech in the "open."

Fundamental values are coming into direct contest. Something will have to give. The question is, what? What are we going to be willing to trade away as a civilization?

There are broadly three possible paths forward.

The first path is that national governments could take broad control over the rules and enforcement of speech on the internet for their citizens, as the Chinese have done. This was historically both unthinkable and impossible, but today it is both feasible and has some clear benefits—along with enormous costs.

The second path is exactly the opposite. We could use new technology to fully guarantee free speech and effectively complete the project of building a new technological medium of speech. That started with the birth of the decentralized internet, but was never properly finished as a platform. This too would be historically unprecedented—societies, no matter how free, have always maintained some form of control around public speech. This option has certain benefits and real costs.

The third option is that we embrace a perpetual, uneasy and painful standoff between governments, centralized internet platforms for speech and the people. This would be an intellectually unsatisfying answer. It would mean that the risks posed by technology to both freedom of speech and safety would be forever present. But it also does have its historical precedence and merits—so long as these three distinct powers can balance each other in a healthy way over the long term, which may or may not be the case.

None of these paths is universally appealing. But the reality of modern technology is that we are being forced to choose.

We are going to have to sacrifice freedom for security, or security for freedom, or live forever in the murky middle.

In this essay I want to make the case for why these are the only three possible paths forward, and why I believe that the path toward technologically guaranteed freedom of speech is the best option we have, despite its obvious and serious shortcomings.

In order to do this, I want to walk through a series of distinct but interrelated topics.

First, I outline a framework for understanding the unchanging universals of how we as individuals communicate. I will distinguish between three different types of communication. And I walk through how the natural decentralized human mesh network of trust functions to propel context-validated information through space and time.

Second, working from that first principle's framework, I will discuss how technology has altered the topology of natural human communication. I will talk through how technology in the general case forces us to construct new frameworks for either centralized or decentralized trust, and then deep-dive on three distinct periods that we have thus far experienced in the development of the modern internet.

Third, I will outline the three possible paths forward given the world as it has come to stand today, and argue why the path of technological freedom of speech is the best option we have—despite the fact that such a path also guarantees a degree of perpetual risk, cost and harm for people.

In the conclusion, I will offer some practical commentary on how to apply this perspective to thinking about a range of immediately relevant topics in technology. Most of us do not have much power to affect the overall direction of the internet and speech, but there are current narratives on which we should hold viewpoints and agitate around. These range from the risks posed by AI moderating human speech to how to engage with the development of blockchain technologies to how to think about developments like VR and the longer-term implications of the European Union's GDPR.

Hopefully this framework can help readers see some reality in the implications of these current developments.

The Fundamentals of Human Communication

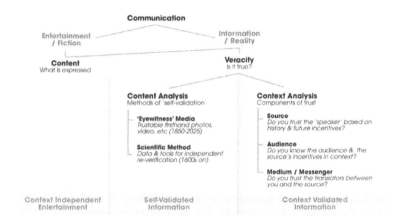

There are two distinct purposes for which humans communicate with each other. We either communicate to entertain, or we communicate to inform.

While today we find ourselves in a muddled content landscape, in the abstract, information and entertainment have fundamentally different purposes, patterns of incentives and methods of distribution.

Entertainment content can stand alone, distinct from any real world context, which is why great stories, literature, music, etc., can stand the test of time. Their reality doesn't matter—what matters is emotions the content evokes in us and whether we enjoy them. For the purposes of this examination, I am going to largely gloss over the details of entertainment content, because its role in the overall story is limited.

Communicating with the intent to inform, on the other hand, is more complicated and more directly relevant to the rest of this proposal. The complexity in information comes from the fact that the content by definition purports to make claims about reality—and needs to be evaluated for truth. To deal with this complexity we, as people, have two different frameworks for establishing truth. We can evaluate the content itself, or we can evaluate the context of the content. These two patterns for validation differ wildly from each other.

Self-Validating Information Content: Firsthand Recorded Media & Scientific Material

We believe the moon landing occurred because there are very good firsthand photographs, videos and audio that seem to clearly show it occurring. When conspiracy theorists claim the moon landing is a hoax, they usually directly question the validity of the firsthand media itself—whether the photos were staged. Our belief (or disbelief on the fringe) in one of the most extraordinary events of the 20th century comes down to an analysis of whether we trust the media generated during the event itself to be valid.

The ability to trust firsthand recorded media is—on a human timescale—very new. Photography is a bit less than 200 years old. Audio and video recording are even more recent content tools. Yet, despite their historical newness, physically recorded firsthand media is a primary tool we use as a society to evaluate the truth of content. Our modern news, information, and democratic governance apparatus is built deeply around our ability to trust source material.

We have been able to rely upon this type of content for the last few generations as a source of truth because it has been too difficult to produce believable forgeries of firsthand content. The only way for the content to exist was for the event to have taken place.

The social impact of recorded content has been enormous. On one hand, it lets us transmit such vivid reality in such a trusted way that it has fundamentally altered how we interact with each other. War was a lot easier to conduct before it was possible to show the world just how brutal it is.

The trustworthiness of firsthand content has also dramatically democratized truth. For the last two centuries, anyone with a camera (and for the last two decades anyone with a microphone), no matter how unknown or untrusted personally, could participate in generating trustable information content because the content's truth could be evaluated independent from the content source.

Recorded media might be our most broad and immediate experience of self-validating content. But it isn't the only place where the invention of self-validating content has had dramatic social impact throughout history.

The scientific methodology, propelled by Francis Bacon in the 1600s, was another watershed moment where creating a framework for information content to validate itself had profound social implications. Before the scientific process, the church held a near monopoly on trust—and by extension had incredible power over people's sense of truth.

The scientific method, which reintroduced the idea of independent verification, effectively allowed anyone globally to produce scientific material that could be evaluated as true. The idea that findings should be presented in a way that any citizen scientist could reconfirm results meant that all of a sudden truth could come from anywhere, not just a few blessed sources.

The challenge is that just as we have become very reliant on self-validating information, this type of information is coming under direct threat from machine learning and AI.

As I have written about before, new technology makes it far too easy and economically accessible for people to create believable fake photos, video and audio recording. I doubt that our ability to trust recorded media alone as a source of truth will survive the decade. We are on the verge of being able to trust the reality depicted by "content" merely because the content exists.

Beyond that, even in the world of science, the idea of self-validating content is coming under threat. If you want to understand the wave of fake science we are experiencing—especially in social sciences—look no further than (1) the fact that the tools and expertise to validate findings are becoming more expensive and harder, limiting the number of people who can validate important work, and (2) even more importantly the fact that data-sets needed to do science are increasingly difficult to access.

Information content that is self-validating has been a powerful modern phenomenon. But while it will still play some role in the future, the reality is that we will look back on it as a historical blip. For most of human history, there was no such thing as self-validating information. In the near future there will be, yet again, almost no information that validates itself.

Contextually Validated Information: The Historical and Future Information Norm

So, if self-validating information is important today, but is neither how information historically worked, nor how we expect information to work in the future, how have human beings established and exchanged information over the millennia and how will we going forward?

The answer is that we are independent, highly tuned systems for evaluating whether to trust information based on the context of the information. This is the "'second" type of information—and is clearly both our past and future.

Think how this form of information works in the physical non-technological world today.

If you are told something by someone, how do you analyze whether to believe it? Likely, you start by quickly evaluating the trustworthiness of the speaker. How long have you known them? Have they lied to you before or have they proven over time to be trustworthy? Are they going to need your collaboration or help in the future which they know they would jeopardize by lying? If they do lie, are you in a position to retaliate with physical or reputational harm (ideally not physical harm in 2018)?

You also might consider who else is the speaker is addressing? What is the speaker's incentive to tell the truth or lie to those people? Will the speaker need the audience's collective collaboration in the future? What power does the audience collectively have over the speaker physically or reputationally? What other relationships or opportunities does the speaker have which would allow them to qualify or modify their speech in the future—with or without you "in the room"?

You might also analyze the medium through which the speaker is addressing you. If you are speaking to someone directly in physical space in the same language, the only question you might have about the medium is whether you heard the speaker correctly. But what if you were speaking to someone who didn't understand English and you were using a translator? Then, you would have to ask, do I trust the intermediary is accurately representing what the speaker is saying? What are the incentives of the intermediary to manipulate the speech of the speaker, etc. (For a very practical historical instance of the importance of this analysis, read Nathaniel Philbrick's book "Mayflower" to learn how much an issue it was for the pilgrims to try to figure out if they could trust native translators.)

The point is this: If the information you are consuming isn't self-validating, then each of us independently evaluates the context of what we are hearing to decide whether to trust what we hear. In near real time we evaluate who is speaking, we evaluate who is listening and we evaluate whether we trust the medium through which the conversation is happening and come up with whether or not we believe what we are hearing.

These are sophisticated social calculations that human beings are very good at doing in real time in the physical world.

The evolved human sophistication at evaluating information based on context for truth is unsurprising. We are not the strongest, toughest or necessarily smartest animals, but we are the best collaborators. We have evolved over the last several hundred thousand years to be very good at these sorts of social calculus.

Before technology, thousands of years ago, we lived in small communities where everyone knew everyone else from birth to death—and families and clans knew each other from generation to generation. We only had to remember a few hundred other people at most. We also had deeply aligned incentives—we all knew we need each other to survive into the future and of course could easily kill or ostracize each other for lies. The incentives for pre-technological people to coordinate and not lie must have been enormous.

Unfortunately, as we will discuss at much more length, the world has become much more complicated. The ties that had simplified our ability to trust what we were told by other people are fraying—at a time where we are going to need to rely on the context of information to drive trust.

The Human Mesh Network: Aggregating, Packaging & Repackaging Information

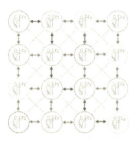

Pre-Technology Human Mesh Network

Information moves through highly qualified and aligned personal relationships;

As network moves information it also 'cleans' it

Thus far we have discussed how different types of content is passed in single interactions between individuals, but we have not addressed how information diffuses through the broader human network.

The easiest way I have found to visualize this is to think of each independently acting person as aggregating information from their physical and social worlds, analyzing it, repackaging what they see as "truth" and then passing that information on to another set of people.

In a naturally functioning human network, we are each effectively "nodes" in a vast decentralized mesh network. We listen to a certain subset of nearby "neighbors" in the network (historically our family, neighbors, etc.), decide whom to trust and what messages to rebroadcast, and then pass information along to the peers who "listen" to us.

In general, historically, we were only connected to a select number of other neighbor "nodes" in the human network through space and time, which meant we repeatedly heard from the same people throughout our lifetimes, knew them and formed well-founded opinions on them.

Because we had these relationships, we had very strong incentives to pass along only what we believed to be truth, and filter out lies and garbage. Each independent person-node in the human mesh both passed along messages and cleaned the network as it went because each person's reputation was directly on the line—and that mattered a lot to the people at each step of the journey. The fact that any piece of content had to pass through countless smart "gates" meant that what did get shared was very high quality.

I see this as a big piece of the brilliance of human communication. The natural human mesh network not only distributes good information, it fortifies it.

How Technology Has Altered Human Communication Over Time

Transportation Technologies
Speed up the movement of atoms (or 'compress' space) bringing new unknowns to the environment

Communication Technologies
Speed up the movement of bits, allowing information to 'catch up' or exceed the physical environment

Social Technologies
'Patch' the difference in speed between transportation tech and communication tech when needed.

So, if we had a well-ordered framework for human beings to pass along truth, what happened? The answer is that technology, for the last several thousand years, has forced us to continuously evolve how we form and maintain our trust in information and shared reality.

Here is one way to think about how technology affects trust throughout history.

From time to time, some brilliant person is able to come up with a new idea that fundamentally improves the speed at which we can as a species move atoms around the world (the wheel, triangular sail, road, domesticated horses, stirrups, steam, railroads, airplanes, etc.). Sometimes we come up with new innovations that allow us to "shrink" physical space between people—such as plumbing, which unlocked much larger towns and cities— which netted out to have the same impact.

When we either speed up atoms or compress the physical space between people, we are suddenly thrust into an environment where there are more unknown new people and things around us with which to interact. This creates new challenges for how we manage trust, and thereby get truth.

There are two ways we can overcome the new unknowns we are put into contact with by technology.

The first is that we can come up with a separate set of new fundamental technologies that accelerate the flow of "bits" to keep pace and keep the world know-able. Communication technologies (writing, printing, the telegraph, phone, radio, TV, etc.) have made it easier to move and access information about new things.

There is, however, an even longer history of human beings developing social technologies and structures to deal with new unknowns. The Ten Commandments and innovations like written contracts, forms of money, nationalization of currencies, establishment of the postal service, the FDA, etc., are all great examples of social and structural innovation that help people digest bigger and more complicated environments to build trust and define truth.

Or, put simply, when we need to interact with new people and there is no basis for trust, we sometimes get new technology to help, but almost always are forced to add social structures to establish and expand trust.

From time to time, new transportation technologies, communication technologies and social technologies come together and allow us to massively expand human welfare. When these three technologies come together we see massive explosions in prosperity.

But there are also countless moments throughout history where one form of technological improvement outpaced the others and led to serious problems and the need for societies to play social "catch-up."

Take, for instance, the era of Upton Sinclair's "The Jungle," where the efficiency of moving food products outpaced the speed of information about the products, and required the creation of the FDA. Or, the opening of the West and the introduction of the railroad, which forced the end of localized banknotes and the creation of a national currency system in the United States.

When you look through history, what you find is that most of these social solutions involve creating a new trusted umbrella organization or brand—a set of easy-to-remember commandments, a religion, class manners and norms, a government, a constitution, "rights," a currency—which everyone can mutually trust. When you can't trust each person you come into contact with as an individual, you find something common to trust and set the rules of interaction.

Sometimes these new trust nodes that are established are decentralized—they take the form of a set of trustable norms—like the Ten Commandments. Sometimes they are highly centralized, like the Roman Catholic Church, with a human organization or even a single person at the center. Broadly, the centralized model is the most adaptable in times of change, and the decentralized model is the most deeply trustworthy over long periods of time.

The impact on human history of social innovations has been massive. But, historically at least, never before has a technology or organization directly subsumed local human physical relationships.

We might have introduced waves of new organizations as part of our overall system, but throughout history—at least until now—we all still had the physical communities around us that we knew, relied upon and shared information with throughout our lives.

The Three Epochs of The Internet (So Far)

Epoch 1 - Raw Web
Unlock new vector of global content movement; new entertainment and self-validating information; **lack of trust & trusted content**

 Epoch 2 - Social Web
Import real world identity & trust to the web; new trusted content brought to the web; **limited content to share**

 Epoch 3 - Post-Social
An attempt to build new digital-only trust and build new content on top of real relationships; **crisis of trust**

The internet is in the rapid process of rewriting the basic rules and assumptions about how we communicate. It is simultaneously changing how we communicate, the incentives for communication and is getting in the middle of historical communication relationships—all at the same time.

No technology in human history has so massively and so quickly affected the fundamentals of how we as humans interact with each other.

That said, at this point in history you can't really discuss the internet's impact anymore as a single technology. There have been at least three distinct eras of "the internet" in rapid succession, each of which added new opportunities—and new challenges.

The Early Raw Decentralized & Untrusted Internet

The earliest days of the internet unleashed a torrent of new content, but somewhat by design lacked the apparatus for establishing traditional trust. This reality deeply shaped the type of content that was originally available online.

The internet was intentionally set up by its creators as an open commons that anyone could connect to and use to share content. It grew like nothing in history because it enabled the flow of all sorts of niche or specific content that had been "bottlenecked" by the traditional physical human networks.

Where the traditional physical human network would effectively screen out and "drop" niche or esoteric content, the internet created an extremely low-cost global vector for these alternative types of content to flow and for alternative communities to build. Some of these communities we see as very good. Some, like terrorist groups, we see as very bad. But the early internet enabled both.

The challenge was, without the ability to represent in a trusted way "who" was speaking or the "audience" that was listening, the early internet was not well set up to generate trust or content that could be trusted based on context. The natural physical memory and incentives that keep communication in check disappeared when anyone could respawn a new identity at will, and content had no context.

As still some of us remember, this was the era of Sandra Bullock in "The Net" and the iconic New Yorker cartoon "on the internet nobody knows you are a dog"—both of which hit on some deeper truth, albeit with perhaps an overly alarmist sheen.

This is why in the earliest days what the internet was good for was generally entertainment, scientific materials and eyewitness content—the types of materials that did not require trust from context. But it was not good for real identity information or the vast majority of trusted content.

The Birth of The Trusted 'Social' Web: Bringing Real World Identity & Trust to the Raw Web

The early web left a clear and obvious opportunity for what became a set of centralized internet companies. Many people recognized that if you could figure out a way to build trust on top of the communicative power of the raw internet, you could unlock all the content that required trust to be shared.

As we know, many companies tried to step in and fill the obvious void, and a few ultimately succeeded.

The way they succeeded was effectively by building a big trusted brand that could tether the internet back to the trusted real world. This allowed them to take advantage of all the natural healthy tensions and incentives that existed around real world identities and accelerate content using digital tools.

There are many interesting and nuanced aspects to how this shfit happened. I will call out just a few of the key "hacks" that took the web from an untrusted and scary place to a trusted one.

First, obviously, there was the move to leverage university-based email systems in the earliest days of Facebook. Universities had, by issuing and validating email addresses, established tiny bridges from physical real-world student identity to the virtual world. But few people used them for anything of much value. Facebook wasn't the first to recognize this opportunity. But it was the first to fully leverage the bridge and use the trust established in universities—for college students initially—to make trusted enclaves of the digital world where it was safe to share photos, real names, addresses, etc. This move made the virtual world feel like the physical one from a trust perspective.

Second, there was the fortuitous timing of the growth in digital photography with cheap digital cameras and camera phones. The university hack would have only gone so far, as most people did not have a trusted bridge to cross from the physical to digital world. But self-validating photography served as a good opportunity. For a while it was too difficult to falsify the number and context of photographs to "trick" anyone about a physical identity. A professional headshot might not suffice, but a few in-context images was good enough for establishing the seed of trusted identity online. Digital photography, mixed with the seeds of trusted networks from universities, allowed the virtual world to match back to the physical one for a far broader set of people.

Third, of course, was the growth and trust in things like phone numbers as unique identifiers. The cell phone companies, coupled with address books, became the "ultimate" if far more permissive university for the world—bridging real world activity to the digital landscape. As of today, when you text someone, or use a service that validates identities via text messaging, you can have context that the virtual representation of the person is tied to the person you intend to share with.

Finally, there were a lot of smart product decisions by specific companies whose impact shouldn't be underestimated. It wouldn't have been enough to simply allow people to prove who they were online with a profile. What worked in this era was a set of product decisions which leveraged identity to make people feel confident in sharing trusted information based on the three key components of trust—Authorship, Audience and Medium.

For instance, in the case of Facebook early on, the original bi-directional friendship model was a brilliant and critical product hack. Bi-directional friendship meant that in order to see something from someone, you also had to be willing to share with them. This encouraged people to make connections only with people they trusted in the real world versus simply connecting to anyone in order to either hear from them or speak to them (as has become the case today). By forcing connections to have a social cost, Facebook encouraged the digitization of only real-world relationships.

In the second era of the web, safe havens and pockets developed, which allowed for trusted private sharing by bridging the relationships and patterns that already existed in the physical world and bringing them online. The exercise of social networking was effectively real-world cartography. It wasn't creating new connections.

Of course, the methodology for achieving this end was not a decentralized protocol or set of rules. It was centralized institutions, and that has made all the difference.

So, at the end of this second period of the internet, there still was the untrusted open web—awash with new and interesting but untrustworthy entertainment content and self-validating scientific media. But there was also enormous centralized private enclaves of sharing, where real-world relationships existed and context-dependent information was shared, with mostly all the same rules and incentives that existed in the physical world.

The Push of The Social Web Beyond Real-World Relationships into New Relationship and Trust Formation

We now live in a third era of the internet. This third era is broadly defined by the move of the centralized platforms beyond their original mechanism of bridging trusted identity from the physical world to the virtual world, and toward using that bridge to support new forms of community and sharing that have no physical world equivalence.

The defining characteristic of this era is the move by large internet platforms from mirroring and accelerating the real world to fundamentally expanding it and trying to bring trust out to new forms of previously untrusted communication and community. Or, to crib the line "software is eating the world" from A16Z, "centralized platforms eat the internet."

Let's briefly discuss why this happened, how it happened and why it has hurt trust in the overall system.

First, the why. Some people believe that this third era of the internet was brought about by some sort of advertising-driven manifest destiny on the part of the large internet platforms. The demand to grow attention and to make money by allowing advertisers to speak to users and create new connections drove the social ecosystem out of control. In my experience however, this is an overly simplistic view.

The real driver of this third internet era is consumer demand. It turns out that people are insatiable machines when it comes to content, and especially entertainment content. Once mobile phones allowed us to be connected to the internet all the time, the human demand switched from efficiency (I only have so many hours at the library in front of a computer, I need to use them well) to expansiveness (I constantly want new, interesting and entertaining content to look at and engage with).

Your real-world trusted relationships can only generate so much content, and the content they generate is only "so" entertaining, so two things happen. First, we look outward beyond our trusted networks to other sources of entertainment, information, etc. We basically bottom feed and start interacting with less trusted sources indiscriminately in search of more content, more entertainment, etc.

Second, there is serious pressure to increase how much each person in our trusted networks shares in order to try to fill the infinite demand for content that we each represent. This leads to a race to lower the barrier to sharing at all costs. If people run out of things to say themselves, a quick re-tweet or re-share experience helps so that they can use the content of others. If people are self-conscious about what they are saying, simply add disappearing media options and allow people to create alternative identities. The product feature list goes on and on to drive more sharing.

The ongoing demand for ever more content— especially entertaining content—could be fine if it were cleanly separated from the sphere of trust and information. But, of course, it is not.

Instead what we find is entertainment that purports to be providing information in order to drive more engagement—despite the fact that entertainment and information have fundamentally different goals. The reason this has happened is largely because entertainment vendors realized that people will only consume so much entertainment content in a given day, but if they think it has social or informational value then they are willing to consume more. This is part of the story of how entertainment has hijacked information.

The second challenge, which is far more dire, is that because of how human beings aggregate and repackage information, once fake or questionable information enters into the stream of good information, it effectively gets whitewashed and becomes indistinguishable from real information. We are used to the idea that when a person we trust passes on information or content, they are doing it in the context of the physical-world rules of the human network—where passing on information has an established social economic cost and implies curation and selection. In the new world however, with the push to make sharing easy and expand networks beyond mirroring physical reality, it is easy for subprime information to get packaged along with good quality information.

So, there is a degree to which you can blame specific platforms and specific product decisions for the era we find ourselves in. But I would urge readers to not take this blame game too far. The reality is that even without these specific product decisions, there is a technological determinism to the place we find ourselves in today based on consumer demand.

At the most basic level, what the internet lets us do is "hop" far beyond our physical, real-world communities and share with people we don't know, with whom have little to no shared future incentives, and over whom we have little to no power . Our demand for ever more content pushes us further in this direction than probably anyone anticipated.

What this third internet era has therefore left us with is a world where we are connected to less trustworthy people and organizations than we ever would have been in the physical world. The value of the human network has almost reversed itself—from being an incredibly good way to "clean" content and refine information to a system that packages together good and bad information and leaves the two indistinguishable.

The Three Possible Paths Forward

Government Control of Speech
National regulation & enforcement of public + private
sphere speech & fragmentation of the internet. **sacrifice
privacy for immediate security**

Technologically Guaranteed Free Speech
Encrypted messages, and 'blockchain' based memory &
identity. single internet, no control of super-empowered
speech. **sacrifice immediate security for privacy & long-
term social resilience**

Never-Ending Tension and Fear
A new normal of deep tension between internet platforms,
governments, and 'the people'. lack of trust in future of the
medium **unclear what happens...**

There are all sorts of counterfactual conversations you could have about how we could have avoided where we are today. I would argue that on the margin the interventionist stance of central platforms, trying to prevent bullying, limiting negative speech, etc., will be looked back upon as an enormous mistake. The same goes for concentrating only on personally positive self-representations of identity versus engaging with the reality of reputation, etc. Decisions like these make platforms and users feel good in the moment, but ultimately accelerate the challenges of the third-wave internet.

Ultimately, we are where we are. Choices were made. The question is only where do we go from here? As I opened with, there are three possible answers, each of which has advantages and requires major sacrifices.

Option 1: Government Regulation and Enforcement of Speech Rules

We could simply invite governments to take over setting the rules for who can speak online, what they can say and the enforcement of the rules they set. While Americans tend to not like this idea, the Chinese seem to have embraced this option, and the Europeans (and Californians) seem somewhere in the middle with the half-step of introducing GDPR (General Data Protection Regulation).

In the extreme, this would mean that governments would issue digital identities, control who could post online explicitly or implicitly through social networks or anywhere else, monitor all communication, set national rules for what can and cannot be said and associated penalties, etc.

There are several broadly appealing components of moving in this direction.

First, we well know that the internet in general, but especially the centralization of power on large internet platforms, is a huge national defense challenge. The future of warfare is manipulating information. We find ourselves today in a place where effectively there are no borders. Foreign organizations and agencies with competing interests can fight all Americans everywhere, all the time, and there is a good argument to be made that good fences make good neighbors.

Beyond national defense, you could argue that this evolution of the internet would make the internet more pleasant for individuals as well. An internet designed like this would likely have very little fraud or hate speech if those things were "outlawed," because it could all be monitored and controlled.

Nationally regulated internets would also ideally bring the people into the process of rule setting—at least if you believe in orderly democracies. It could be well argued that questions about the limits on free speech or where to set the line between public and private speech perhaps should be debated in a democratic forum rather than in private. If we really are faced with new fundamental tradeoffs between freedom, privacy and security, isn't that precisely what national rules and national enforcement are for?

There is also an argument that we as a species are better off with a series of distinct internet spaces versus one consolidated internet. One argument I always like to consider is that, in nature, polycultures tend to survive where monocultures tend to fail. As much as I personally believe that the Europeans have enacted poor and dangerous laws in the case of GDPR, a world where Europe experiments with its own version of the internet is not necessarily bad if you think that it is good for the internet to be a patchwork of experiments versus a single monoculture.

At the same time, the astronomical price we would pay for these benefits should be clear.

First, it would be the end of freedom of speech as a principle. Societies have always put limits on speech in the public sphere. You can't yell fire in a crowded building, and we also limit what people and corporations can spend on elections (which is certainly a form of speech).

What is new about the internet—and especially the consolidated platforms—is that in theory governments can monitor and block what is said in private spaces as well. This is historically unprecedented. Even in regimes that have tried concepts like thought police, there was always the opportunity for free private speech in small groups in the back of bars and salons.

As I have written about before, there is no way that the public and private spheres will stay distinct in the future. There is too little that differentiates a large private messenger thread from a public form. This means that regulation is effectively all or nothing, and we should fear handing over any such absolute power to a regulator. At some point, in some generation, once the power is in place, it will be abused. And technology lets the abuse be "absolute" in a way never before experienced in human history.

Second, it would also effectively be the end of the internet's original dream. A regionalized and factionalized internet, where information and identity need to pass through checkpoints or customs to go from one country to another, would be the end of this generation's conception of the internet. An open and connected world would become a distant historical dream, and we might look back on the world of today much as we do the period of free trade and open borders leading up to World War I.

The question is whether we deeply care about giving up this dream of a connected world. There was something exciting opened up by the freewheeling early internet, and there is a lot of emotional energy invested in our generation toward the vision of what it could be.

You might also argue that certain global threats we face—like global warming—need a single space for global communication. But there is also the argument that the "dream" of such a single space was a momentary mirage. Just because it is possible in theory to hear from any voice globally doesn't make it feasible for people to process the onslaught of speech. Friedrich Hayek a generation ago pointed out the power of the market as an information machine, compressing the infinite complexity of reality into simple prices which people can respond to. What makes us think that we can manage the brunt of human speech without simplifying algorithms?

In the end, on a global level, we as a species are going to experiment with deep government control over all speech—public and private. The Chinese will run this experiment for us regardless of what we do in the West. Not only will they run the experiment on their own, but they will likely begin exporting their internet globally—offering to run their technologies on behalf of other, less powerful nations. Of course, the countries that strike this bargain with the Chinese will be handing over the ultimate power: power over the freedom of their citizenship to communicate. But some may take the bargain, nonetheless, for the sake of national stability and security.

In the West, the reality is that nothing would be easier for the major internet players to do than to hand off the rule-setting and enforcement of speech to governments. It would take a major issue off their plates, and perhaps represent one of the greatest moments in regulatory capture in history. It would be excellent for everyone's bottom line financially. The internet platforms wouldn't need to pay the tax for legal enforcement and small startups would not be able to compete if rules were written that focused on how the big platforms operate. But I believe that the idea of pursuing a route of state-control of the internet and effectively being a "lesser" China is far too dangerous.

The framers of the Constitution never considered things like the rights of individuals to have identities or the right of individuals to freely remember what they wanted to remember. We guaranteed freedom of assembly and speech in the public sphere, assuming that private speech was technically not regulatable. We can't let the possibility of new forms of technological control by governments cloud our overall judgment.

Option 2: Finish Building The Technical Infrastructure for True Freedom of Speech

It is possible today to use technology to fully guarantee freedom of speech in a way which was not thinkable to the original creators of the internet.

In some pockets, this mission is already underway. In the earliest days of the internet, there were serious questions about whether it was legal to allow the use of cryptography online to secure communications. In the early versions of Netscape, you literally had to check a box promising you were an American so the company could not be accused of exporting weapons-grade cryptography.

Flash forward to today and there are secure forms of communication guaranteed by cryptography— ranging from iMessage to WhatsApp—and many groups that take cryptographic free speech seriously.

The challenge, of course, is that you need a lot more than just secure end-to-end encryption to support meaningful communication. You also need secure and private identity, memory, etc.

These concepts are newly addressable, at least in theory, with the combination of public-private key cryptography and forms of distributed immutable memory in the form of things like blockchains.

Imagine the world where a major internet company decided to issue each person on their platform a public and private key-pair as a form of identity. Or, imagine that a startup could get enough distribution on their own to build momentum toward that end.

Everyone could be identified by their public key. Anyone could write public or private "claims" about any other key (signing the information with their key and the keys of intended recipients). And, critically, all the "speech" shared over time could be stored in an append-only distributed database—supported by good cryptography and good economics—that would make it impossible for anyone to rewrite history or limit speech.

People could have as many different identities as they want. In a system like this, fraudulent identities spewing falsehood would abound. But this is the system that would most closely mirror how the real physical world works today, which is its benefit.

Like the real world today, anyone could say anything to anyone else. Anyone could remember anything they wanted. No one's identity could be blocked or eliminated. We would have true freedom of speech, memory and identity.

We would still need centralized services on top of systems like this. It would be too much content for anyone to process or understand in full alone—but all of a sudden the aggregators that point at what information is worth looking at and which people are worth trusting would compete in an open marketplace where the base information of identity and memory was an open and level playing field.

The question, of course, is do we want this? The benefit should be clear.

True free speech online would mirror closely what we have today in the physical world. If you believe that free speech is the bedrock of good government, then technologically guaranteed free speech seems like a critical development.

I would argue that a system like this might also help repair online trust. Today, because speech isn't free and open online, we always need to question what we are hearing. In the technological free speech world, I anticipate you would still have aggregators and feeds, deciding what to include or not include in a given product experience. But the baseline identity and content of the internet would be open and accessible. Anyone could build on top of it or re-use it for new experiences.

A system like that would create a framework where aggregators could compete, and individuals could always go and directly look at baseline "truth" on their own if they wanted or needed to confirm something.

To be sure, there would be a huge amount of junk, lies and attempted manipulation in a system like this, but it would also be reasonably easy and transparent for everyone to evaluate whom to trust, the sources of information and what to believe. You just have to explicitly pick the nodes to listen to in the network, with full knowledge and trust of who they are.

The challenge to a system like this is whether we would tolerate a world where the most abhorrent speech was unstoppable. Bullying would abound. We would have to be comfortable with an incredible amount of deceptive and manipulative speech alongside good information, and use good tools and systems to sort real meaning from useless chaff. Any sympathy to ideas like the European right to be forgotten would have to be thrown out the window.

I personally believe this is a course that needs to be pursued. The fully decentralized internet—capable not just of speech but also identity and memory—seems like critical infrastructure for the future. But it will be painful if we end up here, and more painful still if people try to build this and governments decide to try to stop it.

Option 3: Constant Strife and Tension

So far we have outlined the two possible extreme outcomes—complete government control or complete freedom of speech. There is, of course, a painful third way.

The third path is that we simply tolerate an uneasy tension between regulators, internet platforms and the people for a long time to come. Governments lean on platforms, which are large and powerful enough to lean back (at least to a point). People and their beliefs hold meaningful sway over both, especially in well-functioning democracies.

For those who fear government regulation, and also fear true free speech on the internet, this might not seem like the worst outcome. Many people, myself included, trust the principles and decision-making of certain technology company leaders over the general democratic decision-making process in the U.S., at least for now. I would assume that most people would trust the decision-making of these company leaders over the choices of the worst political regimes on earth.

Even if you fear the scary degree of power concentration that a setup like this would imply, there theoretically could be a healthy balance between governments, platforms and people—where each player has a deep ability to negatively impact the others if they get out of line.

In a sense, this middle road is appealing for those who recognize the problems we face, but are unwilling to accept either extreme possible outcome for the future of speech. If you don't like the security implications of truly guaranteed free speech, and you don't like the freedom implications of national control, then you effectively roll the dice on a solution that might be able to moderate all interests.

The costs of accepting this type of tension long-term though are truly worth considering.

First, to accept this solution is basically to acquiesce to decision-making, on speech and privacy, that isn't inclusive. In a world like this, the primary decisions about speech would not be made by a community through policy mechanisms but primarily by private companies through corporate structures. Policy makers are left to only apply pressure and respond. This is a challenge in big economies like the U.S. where the central internet platforms need to at least respond to governments. But it must feel like a near impossibility in countries with less sway.

Second, we should all fear overcorrection by private institutions into scary outcomes. There is a line I have often heard repeated that the difference between China and the U.S. is that in China the government does the dirty work, where in the U.S. we keep the government "clean" and let private companies do the dirty work for us. If there is even a grain of truth to this cynical outlook, it is that there are decisions that the U.S. government could never get passed which private companies can make on their own. We should all fear this. Even the best-intentioned people make mistakes, and when a lot of decision-making power is privately concentrated without a lot of control, the cost of those mistakes can be extreme.

Third, in a three-party negotiation like this, two parties can usually gang up on the third. Similar to the point above is the fact that, over the very long term, we should fear a world where governments and private companies, through God knows what corruption in the future, gang up on the people in a way that the government alone would have trouble doing. It is reasonable to fear undocumented back doors negotiated in private far more than we fear explicit policy.

Conclusion and Practicalities

I have outlined three possible distinct futures. Individual societies are going to need to choose, but the reality is that we are likely going to get all of them in global aggregate at the same time.

Some governments will opt to take control of the internet within their countries. China has—they will export their technology, and at least some other countries will go down the same path.

Someone will build and release a technological framework for truly private free speech and finish the internet project. How the rest of the world reacts to it is in question, and whether it becomes an illegal backchannel or a central pillar of human communication is up for contentious debate, but such a system will happen.

Likely there will also be an ongoing draining, demoralizing tension strung between governments, companies and people over how our modern speech platforms work.

There may be key moments where a nudge in one direction or the other will have meaningful impact in the ultimate balance of power and where things shake out. But there is no question that this tectonic game will still be slow in coming, and it doesn't leave most people with much hope for how to immediately have impact.

I do, however, want to end this essay on a slightly more immediate note, and address a series of points that fall out of this analysis where immediate action and influence might matter:

The Development of Blockchain Technologies

Blockchains are to memory and identity as the internet is to speech. If we are going to get the trusted distributed system for memory and identity that we need to support context-oriented trust and truth online, blockchains are going to be a critical component.

Right now, much of the conversation around blockchains is obviously about cryptocurrencies. This makes sense. A ledger of balances is ultimately the most compressed and highest value form of information to store. But in the longer term, blockchain's real impact will be as critical technology for assuring freedom of speech, not for things like supply chain management. This is where investment dollars and work should be going in the space.

Artificial Intelligence Content Moderation

If you have any sympathy toward the free speech arguments I have presented, I believe you should be fighting back against artificial intelligence content moderation on Western platforms with full vigor.

Handing over the rules around speech to machines—but especially black box algorithms—is one of the single scariest things we could do as a society. It is one thing for a deterministic digital platform to stand in the modern world between us and those with whom we talk in a new way. The idea of handing over guardianship of the fundamental human infrastructure to machines is a recipe for disaster at some point.

VR & The Hybridization of Reality

While you are at it, push back against VR as well. One solution to the "truth" problem is that we all retreat from truth entirely and focus on building and experiencing our own little personal worlds in VR.

Short of the full science fiction dream of VR disconnecting us from reality, there are several half-steps toward that in process, like Instagram, which are taking us down the path of individually disconnecting from the real world.

I think it would be a tragedy for us all to retreat from each other into virtual bubbles. But it does feel like the move that people might start endorsing—at least those who want to stick their head in the mud given the size and scope of the communication problem we face.

GDPR, California and The Right to Be Forgotten

As discussed throughout this essay, part of me feels happy that different communities are experimenting with different rules for the internet. That said, I do think that the experiments you run, to be valid, should ideally fit within the context of fundamental technological change and our individual physical world experience. My concern with GDPR is that it fails both of those tests.

The blockchain technology coming is fundamentally non-GDPR compliant because the whole point is permanent, trusted, irrevocable memory. Generally, when useful technology and policy cross swords, the technical innovation wins.

Not only is the technology not compliant by its fundamental nature, but neither is the policy aligned with the human experience we live in the physical world. Again, picking on the right to be forgotten and this idea that people "own" their identities—the reality in the physical world couldn't be further from the truth. You have no right or ability to tell me to alter what I remember. The only reason that such a concept—the right of memory —isn't in the constitution already is that no one a few hundred years ago could conceive it would ever be challenged.

In Closing

When the printing press was invented, it was not an overnight success. Many excited entrepreneurs rushed to establish presses, but they couldn't figure out what to print that people would buy. The popular story is that they were saved by the Bible, but the real story is that the first successful product of the printing press was indulgence documents used by a corrupt church to sell years out of purgatory. The great irony, of course, is that church indulgence documents ended up financing the dramatic expansion of the printing infrastructure, which was directly turned against them by Martin Luther in his Ninety-five Theses.

How similar or dissimilar will our era turn out to be? The internet was built on a model of open and free communication, but it is possible that at its current course and speed its ultimate fate could end up being to bring about the exact opposite for humanity.

It is clear that the single global internet of the last 20 years is fracturing and fragmenting. The internet will have different flavors and competitors globally as China expands its reach and governments look to establish, at a minimum, a better seat at the table.

My hope is that we are able to build the technology necessary for a true free speech internet, with identity and memory, and defend its existence through early infancy so that we can have a truly free internet in the future. Without it, I worry we are at fundamental risk as a species. With it, there will be pain, but at least we will have thrown away the keys and created new, deeper forms of trust on the internet's distributed model.

15: How Political Content Fills the Void Left by Micro-Targeting

Jan 21 2019

What if in the near future inequality continues to rise and the most valuable reason to advertise to many people becomes to seek their votes rather than their dollars?

This was the fascinating question that my friend and collaborator Andrew Kortina posed over dinner recently, and I think it is an important question to consider seriously.

THE TAKEAWAY
As advertising of consumer products has become more specialized thanks to the internet, it has tended to favor lucrative, high-end goods. That has left an opening for people trying to influence political outcomes to market to less affluent consumers.

It is pretty clear that the transition from mass media to the micro-targeting of the internet is changing not only how products are advertised, but what products are being created and for which audiences.

At the same time, as inequality grows, there seems to be a strong argument to be made that the value of the attention of those with less disposable income is declining—and that the lowest- common-denominator buyers ultimately are politicians attempting to buy support and votes with increasingly extreme and inexpensive rhetoric.

It is impossible to imagine a move back toward the era of mass media, but it is worth examining the aspects of mass media that we perhaps underappreciated until it was lost.

The Medium Is the Message & the Product

In the pre-internet mass-media era of advertising, the products that could effectively be marketed and sold needed to appeal to broad populations, specifically because advertising was so broad and imprecise.

Brands like Coke, McDonald's, Tide, Gillette, Marriott and Marlboro all worked because nearly everyone could be a customer. When you marketed to nearly everyone in a mass-marketing channel, the effectiveness of your spending could be much higher than a brand that still had to message everyone, but could only be bought by a small percentage of the people exposed to it.

In this era, everything was about converting the people you reached into people who bought something from you. The race was simply to develop ever more mass-market-appeal products that you could market.

The internet changed all that with micro-targeting.

With micro-targeting, rather than reaching out to everyone, you only need to pay to speak to the narrow segment of your exact target customer.

The net result of this is that broadly targeted brands lose, and highly targeted micro-brands can better speak to, and monetize, just their segment of customers, and skip over everyone else.

That means that products that would never have had a prayer of finding an audience in a mass media world, from $1,000 air filters to monthly electric toothbrush subscriptions to pubic hair softener, all of a sudden not only succeed, but succeed better than almost anything else.

In today's highly targeted environment, what actually matters most is no longer the potential conversion rate from views to customers, but instead how tightly you can select the people you want to talk to, and how much you can afford to pay to win each of those individuals.

As the internet has massively expanded the pool of people any brand, even small ones, can reach, and allowed for deeply personalized targeting, the game is about how much margin you can make when you convert someone (which defines how much you can afford to pay for attention from those people), and how specifically or narrowly you can select whom you want to speak to.

Enter Inequality

In some ways, there is good reason to celebrate this movement from large mass brands to highly targeted specialized products. The move in many ways makes products and services better for the audiences they appeal to versus having products that are generally OK for all (such as soft drinks, cigarettes or sitcoms). After all, most of us like our Netflix shows a lot better than what was available on the three major networks for decades.

The problem is that as we get better at micro-targeting, we are also living in an increasingly unequal world. And it turns out that in an increasingly unequal world, capitalism biases heavily toward not only marketing to but building products for the people with the most disposable income.

I, of course, am generalizing, but the big fear (which I believe we are seeing play out currently on the internet) is that with better targeting and growing inequality, the competition to create better goods and services for the richest people will continue to intensify, while the market for everyone else becomes less vibrant because it is harder to monetize.

My strong bet is that because of this dynamic, most innovation and product work in the coming years will continue to aim upmarket, as we are seeing currently with increasingly outrageously expensive smartphones, to name one example. You pay more to reach better customers and skip the customers you don't want versus paying an average price for all.

From Sales to Votes

So, the cynical question is, what do you do with all the now-remnant advertising inventory aimed at those who don't have as much disposable income? When companies don't want to speak to people who can't buy their products (and no longer have to), who fills the void of inexpensive attention?

As capitalism no longer is forced to market to those without capital, and the incentive to serve those populations abates, the buyer of last resort of that attention becomes people trying to influence political outcomes.

It feels very sad, but also fully rational given our current market and government framework that if you don't have capital, the market won't serve you, and that those who talk to you and value you are those who are after your political support.

Late Capitalism

The internet has fundamentally challenged traditional capitalism. The industrial and transportation revolutions did a curious thing to the historical balance of human capital in the last few centuries: It made financial capital far more valuable, and relatively devalued social capital, which for most of human history was the bulwark of civilization.

The internet reverses this by allowing information to catch back up to the flow of goods and services around the globe, and relatively revalues social capital and devalues financial capital.

I still fervently believe this interpretation of what is happening in the world today, but Kortina's insight makes me think that there is an even more immediately challenging way the internet is affecting capitalism, which is that it is morphing the dynamics of capitalism from being something that applied to everyone to something that only applies to a minority of people with capital, and those that flock to serve just them, efficiently excluding the have-nots.

If this is what ends up happening, and populism fills the newly underpriced attention inventory of everyone else, it will be a fascinating and I believe novel lesson in history—and an outcome I doubt even a thinker like Marx anticipated.

16: A Warning on the Dangers of Ephemeral Messaging

March 8, 2019

Facebook's decision to move toward end-to-end encryption and "secure data storage" is the right call. It is necessary. With this decision, company executives will be on the right side of history, as I will explain more below.

The decision to more deeply embrace ephemerality as part of the future of their "privacy" strategy is, however, a mistake.

THE TAKEAWAY
By moving toward full encryption, Facebook can help society guard against central governments trying to regulate people's private communications. But the risk that messaging will become the forum for information warfare suggests that Facebook's embrace of ephemeral messaging is a mistake. Records shouldn't be kept centrally, but they should be kept somewhere.

Driving toward disappearing messages may look good on paper, and may seem consistent with what users think of as "privacy." But I think embracing ephemerality will ultimately prove to be somewhere between regrettable and deeply problematic both for society and the platforms that adopt it.

First, ephemerality is going to prove dangerous when it comes to defending ourselves in the future of information warfare, which will mostly happen on private channels and in living rooms, rather than the "town square." Companies will need data about misinformation to fight misinformation, for example. The solution shouldn't be centralized record-keeping, but local data retention. Records should be kept somewhere.

Second, ephemerality will force a series of questions about ownership of information that we are ill-prepared as a society to address and that I believe we should leave un-formalized.

Finally, unlike encryption, ephemerality is both impossible to guarantee and runs contrary to the natural trajectory of technology. In my experience, when you can't trust something and it runs against the grain of what technology fundamentally does, it becomes a liability.

Why embracing encryption is the right call

There are several reasons that moving to embrace encryption for private messaging is the right call for both the world writ large—and for Facebook as a company.

On a societal level, we face globally an unprecedented consolidation of control over human speech onto just a few platforms. Not just public broadcasting, but literally all speech. There is no precedent to help us think through what that means.

It is almost guaranteed the power we now wield to control private speech will, at some point, go terribly wrong.

It could happen in a variety of different ways—from poor decisions by company leaders to communities advocating for things that are not ultimately in their best interest. The only thing that is nearly certain is that the power is so great, at some point it will be misused, with cataclysmic results—if not in the next few years, certainly in the next few decades.

Historically it was impossible in practice for dictators to regulate living room conversations. They could only regulate the public discussions in the "town square." The fact that all speech—if centralized and unencrypted—can now be monitored at scale will eventually lead to disaster. The only solution for central platforms is to throw away the keys.

If that is the macro-social reason why encryption is critical, it also should not be lost on anyone that moving in this direction is the only way that large international speech platforms will survive into the future.

We largely lived in a "pax digitus" for the first few decades of the internet, where the internet was an "other space" that was left alone by regulators. This era is clearly over.

It will be a hard fight for Facebook to get from where they are today to global, secure end-to-end messaging. Most people have forgotten how controversial the export of encryption technologies outside the U.S. was for the first wave of internet companies, and in many ways this is many orders of magnitude more impactful. But it is the right thing to do, and I am glad they are up for the fight.

Why including ephemerality as part of the privacy narrative is a mistake

It is obvious why consumers "like" ephemeral messaging, and easy to understand from a lay perspective why, if polled, I am sure they view it as a strong privacy feature to have their messages "disappear."

Exploding messaging makes people think they can share more, that their messages will be distributed in a more limited way, in a context which requires less cognitive load and consideration. It feels like they're just shooting the sh*t at a bar where no one will remember what you said the next morning.

That said, it is a very poor idea to treat ephemerality as part of the overall privacy narrative for three reasons:

1) Ephemerality creates serious risk of completely un-auditable private speech at hyperscale

Private messaging is the next battlefield for information warfare, disinformation and subversion.

As I wrote a few years ago in the column, "Free Speech and Democracy in the Age of Micro-Targeting,"the thing to really be worried about is individuals and organizations using the internet to believably and personally interact with millions of people personally and privately, telling them what they want to hear and skipping the "public" sphere entirely.

I do not believe that the answer is for records of private messages to be kept and accessed through a centralized platform. The risk of that centralization is even greater than the risk of the attacks that will come. It is far too easy for things to go wrong.

However, I also think it is a mistake to believe that you want no records kept at all. When the next generation of bad-actors uses ever more sophisticated AI to manipulate people en-masse through personalized targeted outreach, we must be able to reconstruct and litigate what happened.

What I believe should happen is much the way the world has worked outside of the internet for a very long time. Each person who is party to a conversation should have records of the conversations and interactions they have had. When something goes wrong, society should be able to appeal to—and compel with due process—those individuals to disclose their personal records.

I think it could even be a good idea for a central platform to keep some sort of hash of the message to help corroborate the validity of whatever is "discovered" on the device, and perhaps even have formal data retention policies. I trust the distributed partial storage of millions of people versus a handful of centralized platforms.

The pain, cost and publicity of the state getting records from groups of its citizens (or non-citizens!) is far greater than the costs associated with going to a centralized platform, which creates a healthy social tension and balance.

Encryption is a powerful tool. We should have it to defend against centralization. But the idea that we should have no records is simply a bridge too far. Instead, we should trust people to maintain and control their own "correspondence" today, as they have in the past.

Allowing anyone to talk to anyone else instantly, at scale, completely in private, with no ability— under any social or legal framework—to know what is said, is too dangerous even for my taste.

Records are all that allow us to as a society find networks of bad actors, and hold the powerful to account for their speech and actions over time.

2) Ephemerality exposes challenges of information ownership which we won't resolve

If one person takes a picture on another person's camera of a group of people at a party, who owns that image and should have access to it in the future?

The formal legal answer might be that the person who snapped the picture owns it, but in practice that isn't how it works nor is it how we would want it to work as a society.

The same question comes up in a conversation. If we speak together, and iterate on each other's ideas, who owns what utterances? Should I be able to take back mine in the future even if it destroys the context and meaning of your words?

Right now, we live in a world where the idea of information ownership is—on a day-to-day basis—socially enforced and casual versus formally structured.

If platforms make shared media ephemeral, and only permanent to the person who formally "owns" it, more precise definitions of ownership in day-to-day media will be required. That will lead to all sorts of weird behaviors (30 photos of the same thing, copying important notes and conversations and recommendations separately out of a thread, etc.)

In the physical world, ownership may be easy enough because possession is 9/10ths of the law. An object can only be in one place at a given time; however, information is a very complicated system. Information moves by being copied rather than "moved" as we share with each other, and learn from our surroundings.

Moving toward "ephemeral" messaging forces us to start to consider all the social contracts by which we share information and content with each other. I don't think we are at all prepared to tackle the fundamental questions this creates.

We all understand how letters work. You don't ask for them back once they are sent. The same thing goes for email. We all know that you can't force someone to forget something (or ever prove that they have). In my mind, it would be a big mistake to push this form of sharing fully into the mainstream as the norm, rather than the exception.

It will either lead to confusing special cases which will invalidate the overall sense of ephemerality, or will devolve into a set of arguments about context and ownership that are even more complicated than many of those we currently face on the question of "privacy."

Neither of these outcomes are palatable in any immediate sense. The bigger risk is that major platforms make the wrong calls on these things—and fundamentally distort how people naturally interact with each other.

3) Ephemerality is impossible to guarantee and dangerously out of sync with technological reality

I promise you that Kim Kardashian's daily Instagram stories are not actually ephemeral. If I had to bet, hundreds of companies and brands are recording and saving them daily for research purposes. The same goes, I would bet good money, for hundreds—if not thousands—of others.

Encryption is a mathematical ground truth. It is science. If a project is open source, you can prove it. It is true that if encryption is being offered by a large organization that is not open source, then you have to rely upon auditors to prove their claims of encryption - but whether or not something is encrypted is still a fact.

Ephemerality, conversely, is just a product trick. It can never be proven, and if I can see something on a screen, then you can assume that I can be saving and recording it in some way.

Ironically, as the cost of storage and computing declines and the algorithms for reading and structuring images improve, the ability to constantly record everything I am doing will only improve.

It is a big mistake for products to ever "fight" with technology, as opposed to trying to direct it. The idea of trying to enforce memory loss at a time when memory explosion is one of the key features of our society is just out of step.

At some point, people will realize that they can't actually trust "disappearing" messages to disappear, which will undoubtedly be a major future scandal in some form or another.

The best products and product decisions are, in my mind, ones that are able to consider the past and anticipate the future.

Encryption fits well in that narrative. The techniques might need to slightly change over time, but it is a decision for the ages.

Ephemerality is the opposite. It may have existed in a deep, dark prewritten past, but we long ago graduated to a world where things are written down. The historical precedent for it is weak. It also simultaneously doesn't live up to the expectations of any future I can recognize. Except in a world of highly locked down technology or "Men In Black" mind-flashers, it just doesn't fit how humans will want to extend and expand their memory.

If ephemerality becomes a platform feature of the future, then the sad reality will likely be a divergence of the haves and the have-nots, where some people record their lives and have the ability to search over and access it, while others do not. Those who record will have power over those who don't.

The fundamental parts of privacy

The privacy of speech breaks down into control over three elements: identity (who is speaking), content (what is said), and audience (who can listen).

It makes sense that, for Facebook at least, the "identity" part of privacy is left out. It would be a bridge too far to imagine a world where there would be anonymous content on Facebook platforms, both because of the heritage of the company and because people know how nasty and terrible anonymous speech becomes. Also, even I stretch to imagine what anonymous personal messaging actually looks like as a product.

The audience control, who should be able to listen, is the easiest to think about and I think Facebook has it right now. I should be able to share exactly what I want with just whom I want, without having to include anyone else (including any middlemen) in the conversation. That ability to define your audience and freely speak to them is the core of the "living room" experience we need to defend into the technological future for the resilience of humanity.

The content part is where it gets sticky. Ephemerality is, effectively, an attempt to force specific behavior on the content people share— which doesn't make sense. Ephemerality is dangerous given the realistic future of technology and information warfare, it is out of step with how people actually think about information and the patterns by which it is broadly shared, and it also runs contrary to the technological narrative—which is never the side of history you want to be on.

Information moves by being copied from person to person. Technology fundamentally accelerates that model. Products can try to stand in the way of the technological narrative, and might succeed for a while. But ultimately when they collide, technology almost always wins, which is a very good thing.

17: The Future of Free Speech Event Summary

July 15, 2019

Late last month more than one hundred technologists, academics and journalists gathered in San Francisco to talk about the future of free speech. The event—which I organized with Andrew Kortina and Slow Ventures—tackled a range of topics related to how technology is upending how we communicate with each other, consume information and make decisions together as a society.

The event followed Chatham House rules in order to encourage full and open participation. Here were some of my high-level takeaways based on the panels and subsequent conversations:

THE TAKEAWAY

My takeaways on news, technology and communication from a recent event on the future of free speech. **Advertising-Supported Models Encourage Balanced Journalism / Center-ism, Subscriptions Tend Toward Polarization**

In the 20th century, journalism emphasized "balance" in its coverage, reflecting the interests of their advertisers. Macy's, for instance, needed to reach everyone and therefore wanted the publications they advertised in to be balanced and in the center. The challenge of appealing to "everyone" now falls to the large internet platforms, which is why they struggle so much with polarizing voices on their platforms. Meanwhile, as publications like the New York Times move toward subscription models, they are incentivized to appeal to their "base" rather than the middle.

Broad Acceptance of Balance between Freedom and Security, and Fear of Either Extreme

Technology in theory allows for more centralized control over speech than was ever historically fathomable. Technology also allows for scaled private free speech in forms that are impossible in the real world. Either extreme is very challenging to our current civilization, and everyone seems to prefer some form of balance—more than I expected.

The Original 'Internet' Utopian Project is Over

When the internet was young, many saw it as the beginnings of an open global standard that stood beyond the state and connected "the people" directly. That vision now seems utopian. The Chinese have opted out and, in a sense, so have the Europeans. Now individual states and even cities are creating a web of overlapping independent regulation. Everyone seems somewhat unhappy with this, but perhaps it is better for speech, and speech norms, to be somewhat fragmented globally.

Fake News is a Result of Disempowerment

Real news and information is important if you are empowered to make decisions. Part of the rise of fake news might be explained by a sense of disempowerment. If you don't feel like your voice counts and if you don't have control, then content as entertainment can serve you by reinforcing your beliefs and making you feel part of a community.

Freedom to Speak vs. Freedom After Speech as a Function of Identity

The assertion is that historically everyone always had free speech, but not necessarily freedom after they speak. You can have multiple identities online that do not match your real world identity—so you can't be punished in the real world for your virtual speech. The extreme of this would be anonymous speech, but no one will trust anonymous speech in the future, so it is about creating trusted identities that are distinct from your real identity.

Finally, if historically we were only actually concerned with "freedom after speech" because of internet filtering and big data, we should actually be concerned with freedom to speak in the future.

Quadratic Solutions to Power-Law Problems of Speech

Quadratic voting is an increasingly popular theoretical idea for how democracies could better rationalize law-making. The basic idea is to allow people a "wallet" of credits to vote on issues, and enable individuals who care very much about a specific topic—like gun control—to spend the majority of their votes on that one issue. If we are worried about the "power-law" nature of modern speech on the internet—the biggest voices reach far more people today than ever before—we could counterweigh that by taxing political speech based on reach. For example, if you want to reach 10 people you would pay a $10 tax, if you want to reach 100, the tax would be $1,000 and so on.

All News is Paid & All News Serves Whomever is Paying

Hopefully there is a future where different media is paid for by different parties: end users via subscriptions, billionaire benefactors, advertisers and even the government. So long as funding sources are transparent, people need to learn to read better.

Social Norms Are Currently More Repressive than Laws

At least in the U.S., it is interesting that the social norms of private communities and groups are far more repressive to free speech than the law itself. It isn't about fearing or being limited by the government, it is about being limited by each other.

Demonetizing Content is a Cop-out

Everyone gets the game. Leave something up so that those who support it can't say you took it down. Demonetize it so that those who don't support it can't say you took no action. It makes sense as a PR strategy even if it doesn't pass the intellectual test. There is a big split on whether platforms should be more opinionated or not about the content on their services. There are obviously big questions about the implications of asserting editorial control.

Era of Successful "Bomb-throwing" Technologists is Over

The last roughly 20 years have been about building the technology that was possible regardless of regulatory interests and letting it play out. In the next era, technologists will need shelter from—or to align with—other states, regulators and powers. The era of "bomb throwing" is over. Of course, large technology powers might be well suited to protect the next era of freewheeling techno-extremists for the sake of technical progress.

A Challenging Century Ahead

No one really has answers. Especially in a world where the extremes of completely unstoppable micro-targeted free speech destroying truth and central control are equally scary and unpalatable. So the default is going to be muddling through an increasingly complicated set of overlapping and conflicting frameworks for a long time. The era of simple philosophical breakthroughs like John Stuart Mill's Harm Principle is over for now.

A Flipping of Speech Rules the Public & Private Spheres

One thing that didn't come up, but I have been thinking about recently since the symposium, is whether we are going to see a flipping of the public and private spheres of speech. Historically, private speech was unmeasurable and uncontrollable and consistently free across civilizations. Public speech, in the "town square," was what was "dangerous" and controlled differently in different civilizations.

Is it possible that for the future we need to flip these expectations? Might we move toward a world where you can say anything you want in a public space using your real name, but private speech—newly powerful, scalable and targetable—is what ends up being controlled by societies? I have considered this idea before, but it sticks with me more deeply now.

18: The Challenges Facing Free Speech

October 22, 2019

Many people have asked me in the last few days what I thought of Mark Zuckerberg's speech on "free expression," since it is a topic I have focused on so much. I admire Mark's commitment to free speech. He did an admirable job of clearly articulating both some of the nuanced challenges of free speech, and a rational framework for how Facebook approaches the issue—bearing in mind the broad and diverse global audience he is forced to address.

But there are a few key places where my view of the fundamental philosophical issue—and the right path forward—differ from what Zuckerberg articulated. While I agree that we face the legal, platform and social challenges he articulated, I think we face a set of challenges to free speech that are inherent to the technology itself.

THE TAKEAWAY
Mark Zuckerberg did a good job explaining the challenges of free speech and how Facebook approaches the issue. But because of the impact that technology has on speech, I think there are more complex issues. We are moving from a world of

trusting speech by default to distrusting speech by default.

Namely, because of technology we face a world of more "complete" enforcement of rules and laws, compression of historically independent layers of speech oversight, consolidation of gatekeepers and co-sponsors of speech. We face a difficult move from a world of trust-by-default to distrust-by-default.

Simply put, there is a deeper set of technology-driven issues we need to bear in mind when we as a society think of speech and "rule-setting" around expression.

The Broad Strokes of Zuckerberg's Argument

I recommend people read Zuckerberg's <u>full address</u> themselves, but for those who have not and are looking for a summary, here are the major points he makes:

Free speech is critical to a healthy and inclusive society. Over time in the U.S. our conception of free speech has widened, but in times of turmoil, like the ones we face today, there is frequently an impulse to pull back free speech. That is always a mistake.

The internet has generated for people a new set of realities or properties which have both very positive as well as deeply challenging impacts on our society. In particular, the internet has given a lot more people a voice, made information move faster and enables people to form types of communities that used to be impossible.

Broadly, with these changes, we are seeing the emergence, with social media, of a new "Fifth Estate" where people directly express their voice "without intermediates."

The fundamental question is how you balance between free speech and speech that impinges on the rights and safety of others. Facebook's responsibility is to remove content when it could cause physical danger as much as possible. It also has a responsibility to prevent the definition of what speech is dangerous from broadening beyond what is absolutely necessary.

In the quest to do this, there are specific things Facebook focuses on preventing, identifying them through machine-learning algorithms. Facebook is also focused on the veracity of identities—the voices that are speaking.

On the topic of political speech, Facebook does not believe in limiting speech from politicians (paid or unpaid), because the people should decide what is credible in a democracy, not companies. Zuckerberg believes that political ads, specifically, are an important part of voice and that banning them would favor incumbents. And even if you wanted to ban political ads, it is unclear where to draw the line.

On the topic of hate speech, Facebook takes down content that can lead to real world violence. Identifying what content could cross that line is hard to get right, and you have to be careful of unintended consequences.

Looking forward, there are three threats to free speech that we have to face. The first is a legal threat, as different societies and regimes set rules that challenge free speech (we don't want to abdicate to the Chinese internet model).

The second is the danger of how centralized platforms choose to self-regulate. The third is cultural, as people give in to the impulse to restrict speech and enforce new norms.

Select Reactions to the Speech

While I am sure there are some extremists who would disagree, in conversations over the last few days the idea that free speech is critical to democracy and our values as a Western society seems alive and well (God help us if that were not the case).

Zuckerberg's framing of what the internet has "changed" is slightly more controversial, though still not deeply so.

First, his concept that the internet has ushered in the rise of a social-media "Fifth Estate" may well be the most enduring part of his speech. While the term is not new (and it is a bit confusing since "the people" is generally seen as the Third Estate), it is a brilliant framing and elevation of the role of social media in our society.

But I believe it is a mis categorization to talk about the internet as giving people a "voice" rather than increasing distribution. People have always had a "voice." It just didn't historically carry very far alone, and it existed in the context of more localized communities (and those communities' systems of reward and punishment).

As the old saying goes, even in the most repressive regimes "people have always had freedom of speech, just not necessarily freedom after speech." As I will note later, this distinction is quite important.

You can also take issue with how he discussed the positive impact of ideas quickly spreading online— empowering fundraisers, ideas, businesses and movements.

It isn't clear to me that the "speed" of the internet has deeply positive impacts on our world, though it is impossible to slow down communication once it is sped up. The problem with speed isn't just misinformation (as Zuckerberg outlines). It is that we no longer have time to thoughtfully consider options and respond. The faster you drive in a car, the better your reaction time needs to be—and it isn't clear that we are even close to good enough drivers to safely operate at the speed we now find ourselves moving.

I believe that history will judge us poorly on this. Even events like the Arab Spring—which were lauded at the time—will be looked back on as moments where a lot of damage was done because we as societies found ourselves "driving" much faster than our social reaction times could permit.

On Facebook's Role in Speech

Unsurprisingly, most of the discussion among pundits about the speech has focused on the question of how and when Facebook intervenes in speech. On this topic I want to call out two specific things.

The first is about identity.

In the speech, Zuckerberg discussed how the solution to misinformation is to focus on the identity of the speaker, and to force people to stand behind their statements and be accountable. He discusses that Facebook should (and does) take on the role of making sure that accounts represent "real" people or entities: Facebook is removing billions of fake accounts a year.

I agree with this, but there is some sad irony in it. The idea of "valid trusted identity and real names" was the cornerstone of how Facebook worked, in its earliest days.

The original magic of Facebook when it launched was that, by building off of university-validated email addresses, it created a space for college students to feel safe using real names and photos and connecting to each other online for the first time. It is hard to remember back to those "old days" for most people. But in that era the internet was an untrusted and scary place where you would never use real names (remember "The Net" with Sandra Bullock).

Over time, the pressure to grow rapidly, add and grow pages for companies and other organizations, and extend to communities where there was not "strong identity" has led us to a different place. The trust and accountability of the real world dropped off, which is how it became possible to have billions of "fake" accounts created in 2019 which Facebook then had to try to remove. In many ways it seems the goal is now to recover what was powerful about the beginning.

I agree that focusing on real identity and accountability is going to be the path that can bring Facebook back to a trusted place. However, as I often point out, there are likely growth and engagement sacrifices that will need to be made to get there. For example, my favorite hobby horse is that you can't have accountability with Snapchat-style disappearing messages.

The second point I want to call out is about paid political speech.

Zuckerberg's framework around the importance of freedom of political speech—and freedom of paid political speech—has drawn a lot of attention. Many bloggers and pundits seem to believe that the real reason Facebook doesn't want to limit political advertising is for economic reasons.

I don't think that is true at all. I am confident that people can take Zuckerberg's rationale for not limiting political speech at face value.

It is fundamental that it is up to the people in a democratic society to decide what is right. No technology, company or platform should get in the middle of deciding what political speech is permissible (or even what political speech is). The idea of banning political speech, and/or paid political speech, might make Facebook's day-to-day operation significantly smoother. And it might even be good for the stock price. But it would be a massive net-negative for society.

Challenges of the Future

'There is a deeper set of technology-driven issues we need to bear in mind when we as a society think of speech and "rule-setting" around expression.'
The three challenges that Zuckerberg outlines—legal, platform and social—are indeed serious challenges.

On the legal challenges of the future: While self-serving, the argument that the internet is turning toward Chinese platforms (like TikTok) with very different values and perspectives on speech is true. It's also a reason that governments and people in the West should pause before taking action that weaken Western internet powers.

Right now, we basically have two internet "blocks"—Chinese and American. To the extent that Europe and other areas pull away with different regulations and fragment the Western internet, as is happening now, a vacuum will be left that will allow the Chinese framework to take over more of the world. The fact that it is in Facebook's interest to make this argument doesn't mean that the argument is wrong.

On the platform challenges of the future: this also is real. The problem is that small groups of people, not just the leaders, do indeed wield significant power over our highly consolidated speech platforms.

It is unclear how to fully solve this, but there are two directional answers. The first is to "throw away the keys" as much as possible with technologies like encryption. There are frameworks that allow companies to run big platforms but without the power to intervene in how the platforms are used or to modify the fundamentals of speech. The second, more abstract answer, is for companies to make policy decisions and commitments that would be expensive culturally (and ideally financially) to overturn in the future.

Finally, the social challenge to freedom of speech is the most fundamental. There is no question that today we live in a world where "freedom of speech" is more limited by our peers and friends than it is by any technology or law. Our world is increasingly and deeply self-censored to a shocking extent. This might be generational, but to Zuckerberg's concept, the most important thing is believing that someone's right to express themselves is more important than getting one's own way.

Questions Around the Future of Technological Speech

At this moment where free speech is such a central topic, it is worth acknowledging some of the most important issues about free speech in the modern era that were left unsaid in Zuckerberg's speech. That might have been because they are too abstract and nuanced for his broad audience, or perhaps because there really are few good answers about how to address them.

There are four things in particular to call out about how technology changes the fundamentals of how speech works.

First, technology dramatically increases the "completeness" of any laws we set about speech.

Historically, while societies could have all sorts of speech regulations, it was impossible for a society to monitor and regulate what their citizens were saying to each other on the ground, in person, in the back of bars, etc. Speech laws could exist for the public square, but were impossible to broadly enforce.

Moving into the future, any speech regulations or frameworks societies come up with can be nearly fully enforced since our entire communication stream exists in some technological format. A world where everything is recorded, within "earshot" of an Alexa or sight line of a Nest, is something we should be very nervous about, because there will be over time no escape valve for bad laws.

Further, never before have we been in a place where we could block speech rather than simply punish it after the fact. When you can only punish speech after the fact, any speaker can choose to ignore the law and face the consequences. But with newly possible pre-filtering of speech—essentially for the first time ever—we face far more extreme possible future outcomes we should fear.

Second, technology compresses the layers of speech oversight that used to independently function.

At the most basic layer of human biology and abilities, we have always had complete freedom of speech. We fundamentally have the power to say whatever we want. On top of that base reality, there has always been a patchwork of different systems and organizations which manage human speech in different settings. These range from what can technically be delivered on different mediums, government policies, different publications and venues that host speech to social norms in different communities.

The net effect of this historical patchwork is that different types of speech could exist freely in different spaces. What you could say in a certain church was very different than what you could say in a private home, or in a specific community.

Unfortunately, technology is consolidating and standardizing this historical patchwork of speech spaces and oversight because it is erasing space and time, and making everything searchable across all spaces. This will force a set of very hard conversations about speech as a whole versus speech in communities.

Third, technology has driven a consolidation of gatekeepers and co-sponsors for speech.

Historically you may have always had freedom in your individual voice, but your voice also didn't carry very far alone.

In order for an idea to become broadly distributed, you needed to find spaces and communities to not only host your idea, but grow and distribute it along with you. You had to find a gatekeeper and/or cosponsor (depending on how you see things) to enable your speech.

In a sense, those publications, public venues and groups that hosted your speech became directly tied to it, and both got the benefits of association, but also shouldered the risk of your speech along with you.

To be sure, in our modern technologically driven world, you still need collaborators in order to magnify your voice/speech. But what has changed is that those groups can be far more ad hoc than they were historically. The community that comes together to drive a type of speech can—obviously— be drawn from a global audience rather than a local one.

That makes much more extreme speech possible. If you live in the real world without technology and want to express an idea, you need to find people in your physical community to host your speech. Because that community is likely small and reasonably diverse, you have to say things that are acceptable. But with digital speech, you don't have to be so moderate. You can cherry-pick from a global space of billions of people who will give you permission to do exactly what you want.

The cost of co-sponsorship is lower with digital speech. If you own a physical venue or publication, you have capital and reputation at risk when you host speech. When you have formed an inexpensive ad hoc community to promote your speech, there is no fixed risk you are taking. This changes the nature of discourse.

Fourth and finally, technology moves us from a world of trust-by-default to non-trust-by-default.

We have for the last few centuries been able to—largely by default—trust the people we interact with and the media we see.

The reason we could trust media was that—for at least the last few hundred years—it was very hard to convincingly falsify. This is obviously not the future we will live in. As I have written about before, we are going to have to go back to network-based-trust versus content-based trust.

The reason we could largely trust people was that we knew who they were, and would see them again or need to interact in the future. This has certainly changed with urbanization, etc., but if you think of a small town or neighborhood, the reason you can trust your neighbors is that you know where they live and life is an iterated game. This too is breaking down both as we globalize and as identity becomes relatively more fluid online.

We can't fix the former. We are going to have to get used to a world where when we see something without context we by default do not believe it. This means we have to build better identity and reputation systems so we can trust specific people and relationships over the long term.

Conclusion

We are going to get through this period in history and come out stronger. But I think that we are going to have to confront some hard truths and make some painful choices along the way.

I am worried that regardless of the best intentions of company leaders, regulators and community members, the fundamental technology of the internet moves us inexorably in a direction of more speech regulation than is healthy for the long-term resilience of our civilizations globally.

Once something becomes possible, it takes an almost Herculean effort to not take advantage of it.

If the story of the last decade or so of technology is that speech monitoring and control is now possible in a new way, I fear that the only solution to preserve free speech is technological tools around distribution and encryption that would level the playing field.

www.ingramcontent.com/pod-product-compliance
Lightning Source LLC
LaVergne TN
LVHW041211050326
832903LV00021B/575